NATIONAL GEOGRAPHIC

OUR WORLD

STUDENT BOOK 5A

Series Editors
JoAnn (Jodi) Crandall
Joan Kang Shin

Author
Ronald Scro

NATIONAL GEOGRAPHIC LEARNING | CENGAGE Learning

Australia • Brazil • Japan • Korea • Mexico • Singapore • Spain • United Kingdom • United States

NATIONAL GEOGRAPHIC

OUR WORLD

Let's sing! TR: B41

This is our world.
Everybody's got a song to sing.
Each boy and girl.
This is our world!

I say "our," you say "world."
Our!
World!
Our!
World!

I say "boy," you say "girl."
Boy!
Girl!
Boy!
Girl!

I say everybody move...
I say everybody stop...
everybody stop!

This is our world.
Everybody's got a song to sing.
Each boy and girl.
This is our world!

Student Book:

Unit 1 Extreme Weather 4
Unit 2 Copycat Animals 20
Unit 3 Music in Our World 36
Unit 4 Life Out There 56
Unit 5 Arts Lost and Found 72
Irregular Verbs 160
Cutouts 161

Workbook:

Unit 1 Extreme Weather 2
Unit 2 Copycat Animals 14
Unit 3 Music in Our World 26
Unit 4 Life Out There 42
Unit 5 Arts Lost and Found 54
Additional Activities 122

My Words
Student Book Stickers

Unit 1

Extreme Weather

In this unit, I will . . .

- talk about types of extreme weather.
- describe the damage storms can cause.
- identify ways to prepare for extreme weather.
- write a personal narrative.

Check T for *True* and F for *False*.

1. The temperature is freezing cold. Ⓣ Ⓕ
2. This person is walking carefully on the ice. Ⓣ Ⓕ
3. There was a hurricane. Ⓣ Ⓕ
4. The trees are covered with ice. Ⓣ Ⓕ

Versoix, Switzerland

1 Listen and read. TR: A2

2 Listen and repeat. TR: A3

We know we can't control the weather. It can be beautiful, wild, and dangerous, often all at the same time. Scientists try to predict weather in different ways. They tell us when extreme weather is coming. Then we can try to protect ourselves.

Thunderstorms bring heavy rain with loud **thunder** and **lightning.** If too much rain falls in a short time, it can cause a **flood.** Too little rain makes the land dry and can cause a **drought.** When it's very cold, a rainstorm can turn into an **ice storm** or a **blizzard.**

a hurricane

a sandstorm

Wind is a dangerous force. In a **tropical storm,** the wind **speed** can be more than 100 kilometers (60 miles) per hour. Wind in a **hurricane,** or cyclone, is even faster.

A **tornado** is a column of wind that rotates very fast. High winds in dry places such as deserts can pick up sand and cause a **sandstorm.**

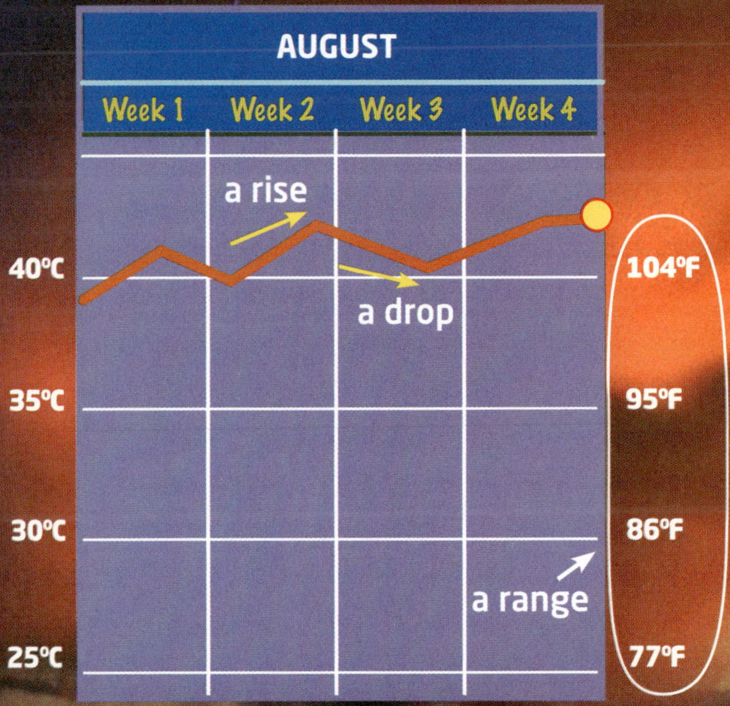

We can only live within a specific **range** of temperatures. At times, temperatures **rise** too high or **drop** too low. It not only feels bad, it can be dangerous! In a **heat wave,** the weather stays very hot for days or even weeks.

3 **Work with a partner.** What did you learn? Ask and answer.

4 **Listen, read, and sing.** TR: A4

Bad Weather

There's bad weather on the way!
There's bad weather on the way!

Is it going to storm? Yes, it is!
Is there going to be lightning? Yes, there is!
Is there going to be thunder? Yes, there is!

When there's going to be a storm, I hurry inside!

Be prepared for emergencies.
It's always good to be safe. You'll see!
Grab supplies and a flashlight, too.
Seek shelter. It's the safe thing to do!

Is there going to be a blizzard? Yes, there is!
Is there going to be an ice storm? Yes, there is!
Is it going to be cold? Oh, yes it is!

If there's going to be a blizzard, I hurry inside!

Be prepared for emergencies.
It's always good to be safe. You'll see!
Grab supplies and a flashlight, too.
Seek shelter. It's the safe thing to do!

Is there going to be a hurricane? Yes, there is!
Is the wind going to howl? Yes, it is!
Are the waves going to rage? Yes, they are!

If there's going to be a hurricane, we evacuate!

Be prepared for emergencies.
It's always good to be safe. You'll see!
Grab supplies and a flashlight, too.
Seek shelter. It's the safe thing to do!
Seek shelter. It's the safe thing to do!

5 **Work with a partner.** Ask and answer.

1. What bad storm in your town do you remember?
2. What did you do to prepare?
3. What did you think and feel during the storm?

GRAMMAR TR: A5

Is it **going to** rain tomorrow? No, it's **going to** snow tomorrow.
I'm **going to** listen to the weather report at 8:00.
He's **going to** put on his snow boots.

6 **Write.** What is the weather going to be like?

Sunday

Monday

Tuesday

Wednesday

Thursday

Friday

1. It's going to be sunny on Sunday.
2. ______
3. ______
4. ______
5. ______
6. ______

7 **Work with a partner.** Read. Ask and answer. Take turns.

1. Why can't we go to the park tomorrow? (rain)
2. Won't she get wet walking in the rain? (take an umbrella)
3. Why is she closing the windows? (rain)
4. When will he get a new rain coat? (today)

8 **Write.** What are you going to do? Write sentences.

A thunderstorm is coming. ______________________________

____

____

____

A heat wave is coming. ______________________________

____

____

____

A hurricane is coming. ______________________________

____

____

____

9 **Work with a partner.** What about you? Talk about today and tomorrow. Ask and answer.

10 **Listen and repeat.** Then read and write. **TR: A6**

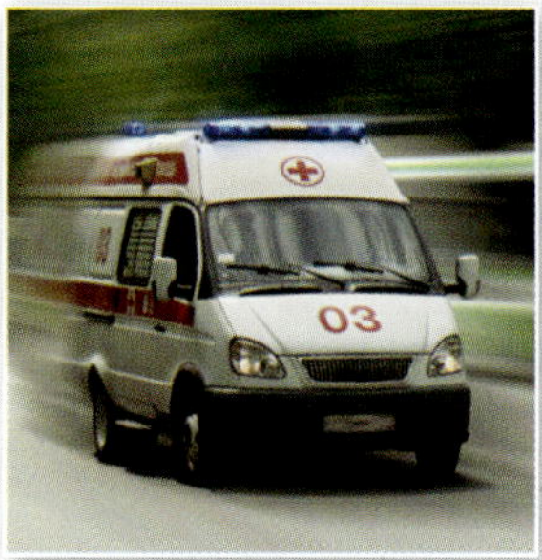
an emergency

a plan

a flashlight

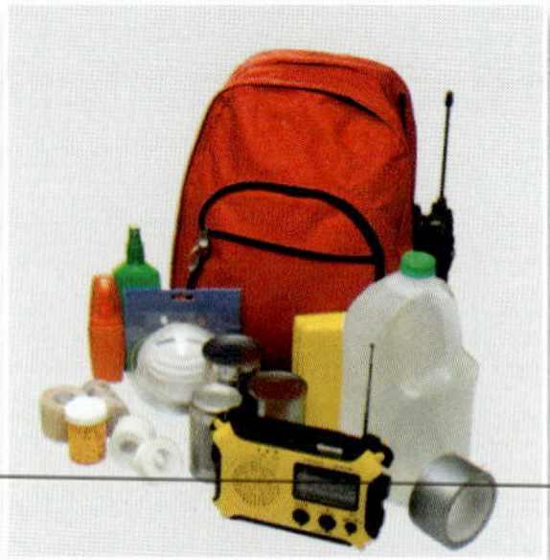
supplies

evacuate

a shelter

When a weather forecaster predicts bad weather, you can make a ________________ to prepare. To protect yourself from wind and rain, you should go to a ________________. If the electricity goes off, use a ________________ to see in the dark. You can store ________________ in a safe place so that you have food to eat. A really bad storm can affect the whole town. In an ________________ like that, people have to ________________ and go where it is safer.

11 **Listen and stick.** Find out what to do next. Place your stickers in the correct order. Work with a partner. Summarize the weather report. **TR: A7**

A hurricane is coming. It's an emergency.

Yes, I put emergency in number 1. That's correct.

1	2	3	4	5

GRAMMAR TR: A8

If the weather **is** cold, I **put on** my winter coat.
If I **see** lightning, I **go** inside.
If a sandstorm **comes,** I **close** all the windows.

12 **Match and make logical sentences.** Then write five sentences of your own in your notebook.

I see lightning when I'm swimming	I look for a boat
it rains	I wear gloves and boots
a storm comes	I try to stay cool
the temperature rises	get out of the water
a flood comes	go inside the house
it snows	I carry an umbrella

13 **Play a game.** Cut out the cards on page 161. Play with a partner. Take turns. Match and make sentences. Keep the cards.

14 **Listen and read.** TR: A9

Tornado Trouble

Tornadoes happen all over the world. There's even a place called Tornado Alley. Josh Wurman studies extreme weather. He joined a team of other scientists to study tornadoes in Tornado Alley. One day, the blue sky turned black. A giant cloud came toward the team. The cloud had winds that moved in a circle. Inside his truck, Wurman watched the storm through his window and on his instruments. Colors on the computer screen showed where the rain fell and where the wind was the strongest.

The winds twisted the storm tighter and tighter into the shape of a funnel. When the funnel touched the ground, it became a tornado! The tornado looked like a giant, gray elephant's trunk. It moved one way, then another way. As the tornado moved across the ground, the team came dangerously close. They dropped special instruments close to the storm. These instruments showed wind speed, temperature, and how much rain was falling.

The tornado twisted and moved for half an hour. The team watched the storm and their instruments the whole time. Then the tornado leaned over slowly like a soft rope. Poof! It was gone. The excitement was over. But Wurman and his team have a lot more work to do. The information from their instruments will help them predict other tornadoes so that they can warn people and save lives.

weird but true It once rained frogs on a town in Serbia. A small tornado dropped them there.

15 **Work in groups of three.** Discuss and answer the questions.

1. What is the shape of a tornado?
2. Where does a funnel touch to become a tornado?
3. Why do scientists study tornadoes?
4. What do scientists use to learn about tornadoes?

16 **Work with a partner.** How does a tornado form? Match the text to each step. Discuss.

a. Warm and cold air currents twist winds into a funnel. Then the funnel touches the ground.

b. Warm air and cold air come together. They make a twisting wind of air that moves in circles.

c. The twisting air stands up. Warm air moves up. Cold air moves down.

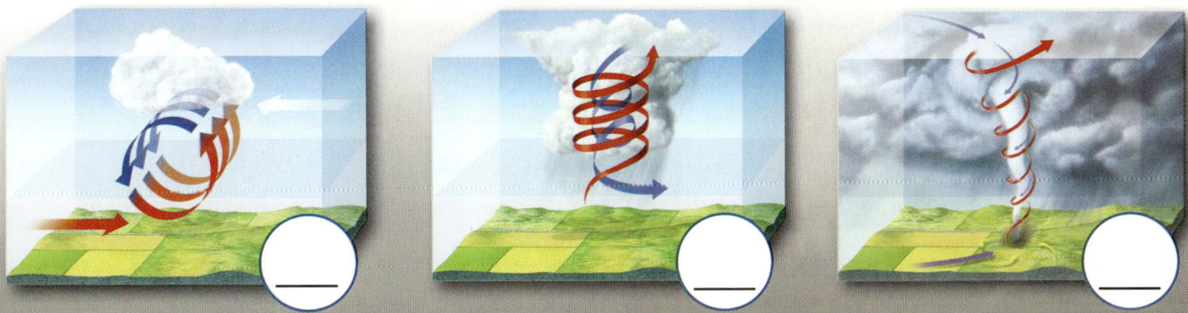

17 **Work with a group.** Compare tornadoes and hurricanes. Discuss. Complete the chart.

Tornado	Hurricane
	Origin: They form over water. Duration: They last a week.

Personal Narrative

A personal narrative tells a story. It describes something that happened. A good writer describes details using the senses—sight, sound, taste, smell, and touch. Readers should feel like they were really there. You can use words like *after, before, next,* and *then* to show the sequence of events.

18 **Read.** Read the personal narrative. How does the writer describe the hurricane? How does the writer describe what she hears and sees? How does she feel? Circle the words that relate to the senses and emotions. Underline the words and expressions that show the sequence of events.

Safe not Sorry!

Last year, the weather forecaster told us that a hurricane was coming. A hurricane is always scary, but a little exciting, too. When a hurricane comes, we know what to do. We have a family plan. First, I had to help my dad put heavy wood over the windows. It was hard work.

When the hurricane came, we could hear the strong winds outside. We could hear the rain coming down hard. Then suddenly we heard a really loud noise. And then something hit our house really hard! Everyone was worried. What could it be? After the storm, we walked outside. Part of a tree hit the wood on the window. I am so happy we covered the windows! Next time, I won't say the wood is too heavy.

19 **Write.** Write about an extreme weather experience. Give details using the senses. Help the reader feel what you felt.

20 **Work in a small group.** Share your writing.

NATIONAL GEOGRAPHIC

Mission

Understand Weather.

- Why is it important to understand weather? Work in a group. Discuss.
- How can you learn more about extreme weather?
- What do you do in dangerous weather? Write your ideas in the box.

- Share your ideas with another group. Are they the same or different? Decide which ideas everyone thinks are best.

"It all started when I was about six years old and saw that fantastic tornado in The Wizard of Oz.*"*

Tim Samaras

Severe Storm Researcher

Emerging Explorer

Storm chasers, Oklahoma, USA

21 Find out how windy it is.

1. Work in small groups to make a wind speed indicator.
2. Make an X with two pieces of cardboard. Staple it.
3. Staple one paper or plastic cup to each of the four ends.
4. Color one of the cups with a marking pen.
5. Push a push pin in the center of the X.
6. Push the pin into a pencil eraser.
7. Hold the pencil up and count the turns in one minute.

The faster the cups turn, the windier it is!

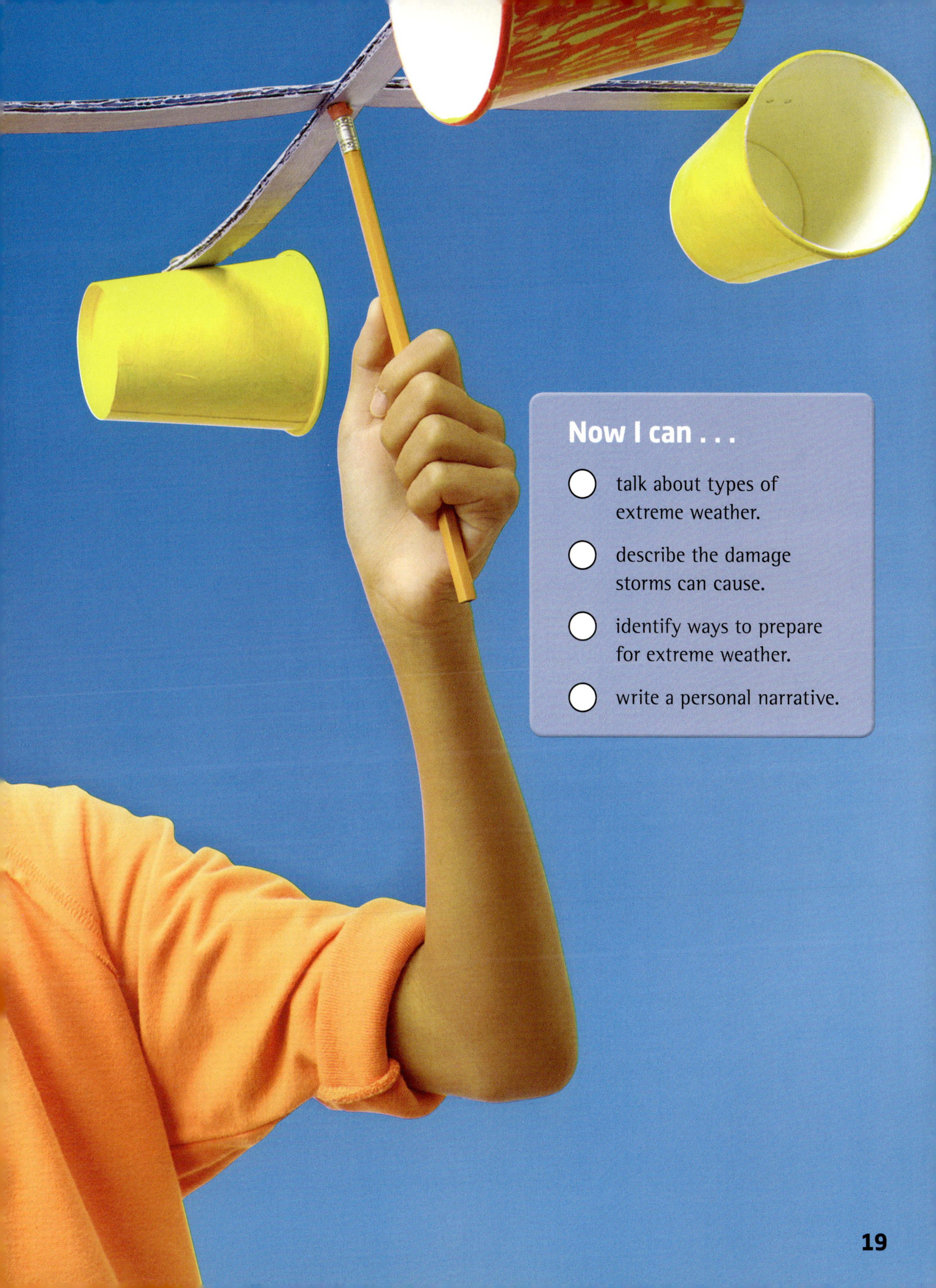

Now I can . . .

- ◯ talk about types of extreme weather.
- ◯ describe the damage storms can cause.
- ◯ identify ways to prepare for extreme weather.
- ◯ write a personal narrative.

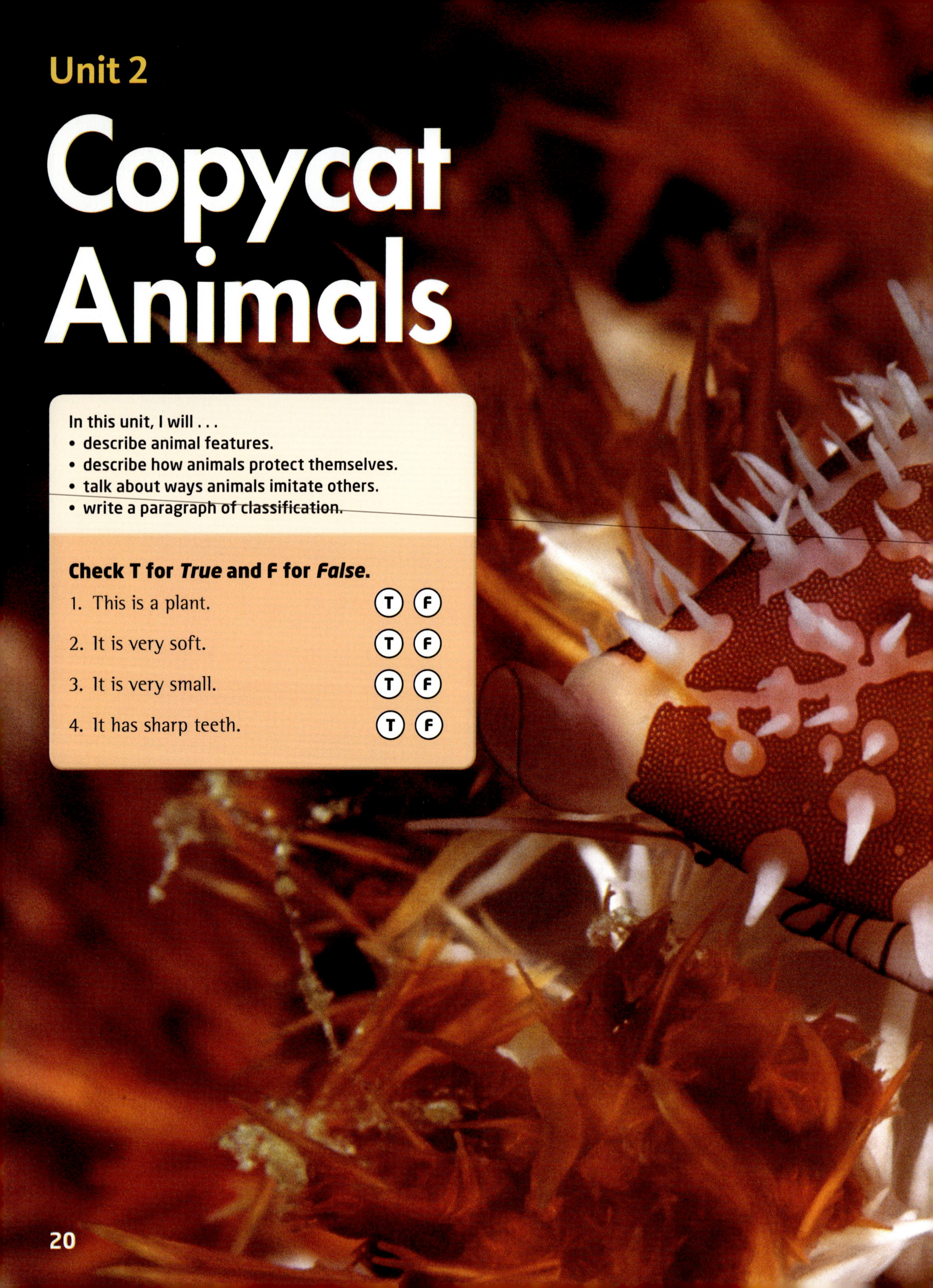

Unit 2

Copycat Animals

In this unit, I will . . .
- describe animal features.
- describe how animals protect themselves.
- talk about ways animals imitate others.
- write a paragraph of classification.

Check T for *True* and F for *False*.

1. This is a plant. T F
2. It is very soft. T F
3. It is very small. T F
4. It has sharp teeth. T F

Allied cowrie,
Papua New Guinea

1 **Listen and read.** TR: A10

2 **Listen and repeat.** TR: A11

Some animals can look like other animals or even like a plant! These copycats are trying to hide from or trick a hungry **predator.** They can look like another more dangerous animal or like another animal the predator doesn't like to eat.

This cheetah's black **spots** act as **camouflage.** This way, the cheetah doesn't **frighten** its **prey** when it's time to **hunt.**

This colorful frog has **stripes** on its skin. The bright colors tell hungry predators that the frog is **poisonous.**

These butterflies are not the same **species,** but they **resemble** each other. The top one tastes bad. The other one **copies** its shape and colors, and tastes bad, too.

This **insect** is as green as a leaf. It **imitates** the **characteristics** of color and shape of leaves to help it **hide** from predators.

3 **Work with a partner.** What did you learn? Ask and answer.

4 Listen, read, and sing. TR: A12

It's a Wild World

It's a wild world!
It's work to stay alive!
Animals do amazing things
in order to survive.

An insect that looks like a leaf
copies plants to get relief.
Predators are everywhere,
and looking for a feast!

CHORUS

Camouflage and imitate.
Resemble and escape!
Animals hide in front of our eyes, every day.

The hunter and the hunted,
predator and prey,
must hunt or hide to stay alive,
each and every day.

A pretty frog can be as deadly as a snake.
Its stripes tell its enemies
"You'd better stay away!"

CHORUS

It's a wild world!

5 Work with a partner. Ask and answer.

1. What predators have you seen?
2. What is their prey?
3. How does the prey avoid predators?

Lionfish, Indonesia

GRAMMAR TR: A13

That katydid is **as green as** the leaf it sits on.
That butterfly is not **as pretty as** the blue one.
Poison dart frogs are **as dangerous as** some snakes.

6 **Read and write.** Work with a partner. Take turns. Compare.

1. some insects / thin / sticks

____

2. a polar bear / white / snow

____

3. king snakes / not dangerous / coral snakes

____

4. a bee sting / bad / a wasp sting

____

5. a lion / not loud / a howler monkey

____

a bee

a wasp

7 **Compare the animals.** Choose one word from each group. Make sentences.

8 **Work in a group.** Take turns. Make sentences. Use the last word in each sentence to start the next sentence.

9 **Listen and repeat.** Then read and write. TR: A14

The butterfly fish **confuses** its predators with a spot like an eye.

The jaguar **attacks.**

The cobra **defends** itself. The mongoose **avoids** its bite.

The deer **escapes** by running away.

1. All predators ____________________ prey.
2. Bluebirds ____________________ their eggs from predators.
3. Calabar pythons have tails that look like heads. This ____________________ predators so they will not know where to strike!
4. Some animals use camouflage to ____________________ predators.
5. A rabbit that runs fast can ____________________ the coyote that chases it.

10 **Listen.** Stick *True* or *False*. Work with a partner. Compare your answers. TR: A15

The spot on the tail looks like an eye. The sentence is true.

You are right! My turn.

1	2	3	4	5

GRAMMAR TR: A16

The jaguar **is** dangerous, **isn't it?**
Those snakes **are** scary, **aren't they?**
This insect **looks** like a stick, **doesn't it?**
Giraffes **don't** eat meat, **do they?**
That frog **wasn't** poisonous, **was it?**
The cat **escaped** the dog, **didn't it?**
The dogs **were** loud, **weren't they?**
The cats **weren't** friendly, **were they?**

11 **Read.** Complete the sentences.

1. The katydid is pretending it's a leaf, ______________________?
2. The donkey doesn't look thirsty, ______________________?
3. That python really confused its predator, ______________________?
4. Cats like sleeping in the sun, ______________________?
5. Baby penguins are so cute, ______________________?
6. Those weren't copycat animals, ______________________?

12 **Play a game.** Cut the question tags on p. 163. Glue nine to complete your game. Listen. Which tag completes the sentence? If you have it, draw an X on the square. TR: A17

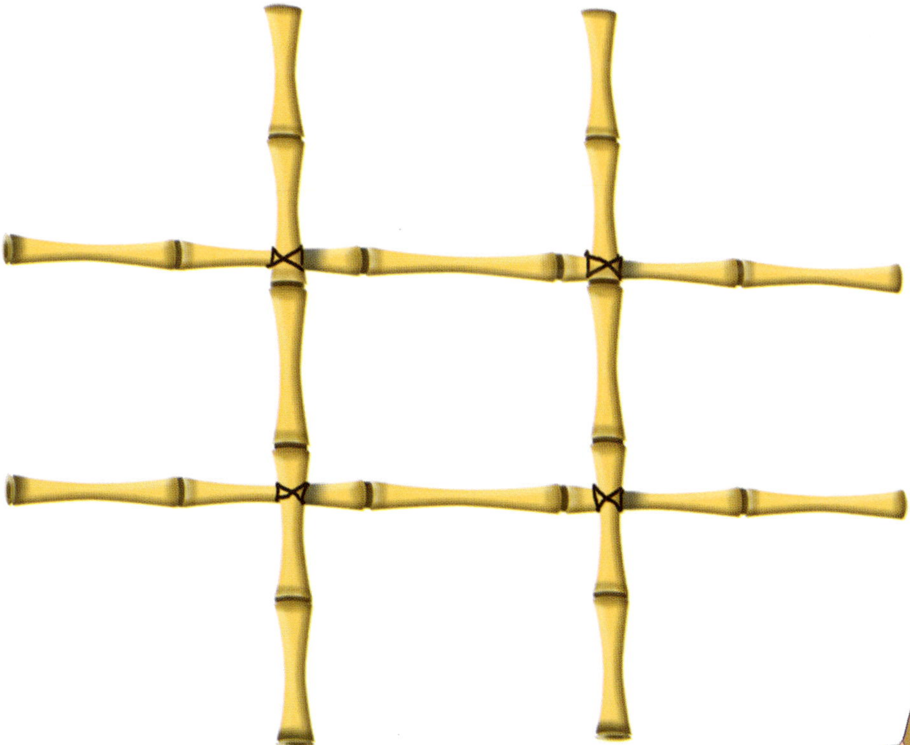

13 **Listen and read.** TR: A18

Copycats

The leafy sea dragon is a weird but beautiful copycat. From its name you would think it imitates a dragon, wouldn't you? But no, it only gets that name from its funny shape. The leafy sea dragon imitates what is around it. It lives in seaweed, and so its body looks like a seaweed leaf. The sea dragon imitates the shape and color of seaweed, and it even looks like floating seaweed when it moves. It doesn't use the parts of its body that look like a leaf to swim. It uses fins that are transparent, so it's hard to see them move.

The leafy sea dragon does not only look like a copycat. It also dances like a copycat. A male and female sea dragon will copy each other's movements for hours!

The mimic octopus is the only sea creature that can imitate many different species. It not only changes its color, it also changes its shape. It has arms as thick as pencils. When it spreads them wide, they look like the spines of a lionfish. It can hide some of its arms in the sand but leave two arms out. Then with its white and brown stripes and the two arms, it looks like a sea snake! It can also pull its arms together and swim on the sea floor, so to a predator, it looks like a poisonous flatfish!

Like other octopuses, the mimic octopus has eight arms and three hearts. It swims by shooting out jets of water through a siphon. It also has a large brain for its size. That's one smart octopus!

weird but true

One kind of spider tricks predators by imitating an ant. It holds two legs up to look more like an ant when it walks.

A mimic octopus imitating a poisonous flatfish

leafy sea dragon

14 **Read and write.** Work with a partner. Compare your answers.

1. What does the leafy sea dragon imitate? ____________________
2. What does the leafy sea dragon use to swim? ____________________
3. What does the mimic octopus look like? ____________________
4. What does the mimic octopus do with its arms? ____________________

15 **Work with a partner.** Choose the leafy sea dragon or the mimic octopus to talk about. Your partner will listen and complete the first row. Then listen to your partner and fill in the second row.

Habitat	Shape	Color	Movement

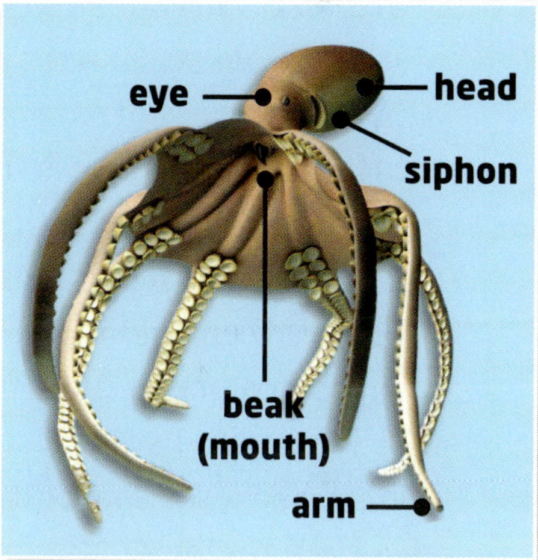

An octopus

16 **Work in groups of three.** Take turns. Summarize the reading.

Paragraphs of Classification

A paragraph of classification describes characteristics that members of a group share. You can define, compare, and contrast details to show how things belong to a group or class. You can use words such as *both, each of, like, but,* and *unlike.*

17 **Read.** Read about two types of copycat animals. How does the writer classify them? What words does the writer use to show their characteristics? Underline the words and expressions.

One or Two Ways to Imitate

Some animals copy other animals to avoid attack. They copy the things that predators avoid, such as a bad taste or a dangerous weapon. Some species copy the appearance of another animal, but not other characteristics. For example, the viceroy and the soldier butterfly resemble each other. They also both taste bad to predators. These types of animals imitate in two ways. The ash borer moth looks like a wasp, but it doesn't have a stinger. Predators avoid it, but it can't sting them. The ash borer moth belongs to the class of animals that only copies appearance.

viceroy butterfly

ash borer moth

18 **Write.** Write about animals that belong to a certain type. Describe the characteristics that they share.

19 **Work in a small group.** Share your writing.

NATIONAL GEOGRAPHIC

Mission

Protect biodiversity.

- Why is it important to preserve diverse species of animals?
- How does biodiversity affect your community?
- Work in a small group. Discuss a local species of animal. Think of ways to protect it. Discuss and write the best ideas in the box.

- Work with another group. Share your ideas. Are they the same or different? Which ideas does everyone like best?

"We need to increase people's interest and awareness about wildlife and conservation issues and reduce the general disconnect from nature."

Krithi Karanth

Conservation Biologist

Emerging Explorer

tarsier

20 Make a classroom mural.

1. Work in small groups. Choose a habitat such as an ocean, a forest, or a desert.
2. Discuss how animals protect themselves in that place.
3. In your part of the mural, show some animals that use camouflage and some that survive in other ways.

There is a leaf-tailed gecko on a tree trunk in the rain forest. It uses camouflage to survive. Can you see it?

Now I can . . .

- ◯ describe animal features.
- ◯ describe how animals protect themselves.
- ◯ talk about ways animals imitate others.
- ◯ write a paragraph of classification.

Unit 3

Music in Our World

In this unit, I will . . .
- identify musical instruments.
- talk about musical styles.
- express preferences.
- write a paragraph of contrast.

Circle the correct answer.

1. The man is holding

   a. a hunting tool.

   b. a musical instrument.

2. He is playing

   a. traditional music.

   b. classical music.

Makena Beach, Maui

1 Listen and read. TR: A19

2 Listen and repeat. TR: A20

There are three main types of musical instruments. String instruments make music when you pluck the strings. Wind instruments make sounds when you blow air through them. Percussion instruments make different sounds when you hit them or shake them.

Music has its own language. Each single sound is a **note.** Play two notes or more at one time to make a **chord.** A string of notes and chords played one after the other makes a **melody.** The thump, thump, thump that makes you want to dance is the **beat.** Combine them all, slow and fast over time, and you have **rhythm.**

a guitar

a flute

a drum

Do you want your **band** to play better? You have to **practice!** Play songs again and again until they sound really good. When your band sounds good, you can **perform** for an audience. Invite your friends to the **concert!** If you don't play an instrument but you have a good voice, you could be the **lead singer!**

3 **Work with a partner.** What did you learn? Ask and answer.

4 Listen, read, and sing. TR: A21

Music Is Fun

Have you ever listened to hip-hop?
Have you ever listened to drums?
I listen to all kinds of music.
It's amazing fun.

Listen to the saxophone.
Listen to the beat.
Listen to the melody.
Feel it in your feet!

The flute is playing.
The piano is, too.
I can hear the guitar.
Can you?

CHORUS

Listen to the rhythm.
Listen to that band!
Sing the notes (la la la)
and clap your hands.

Have you ever played a note?
Have you ever played a chord?
Have you ever played a rhythm:
1, 2, 3, 4?

CHORUS

5 **Work with a partner.** Ask and answer.

1. Who are your favorite musicians?
2. What instruments do they play?
3. Why do you like their music?

Drummers, Ninga, Burundi

GRAMMAR TR: A22

Have you **ever listened** to hip-hop?	Yes, I **have.**
Have you **ever danced** to hip-hop?	No, I **haven't.**
Have you **ever been** to a concert?	No, I **never have.**
Has Lisa **ever heard** an orchestra perform?	No, she **has never heard** an orchestra perform.

6 **Read.** Complete the sentences.

1. This song is new. I ___have never heard___ (hear) it before.
2. I ______________ (go) to see an opera. I don't think I'd like it.
3. ______________________ (listen) to jazz? Yes, I like it!
4. If you ______________ (hear) her sing, then you know she sings well.
5. This is his first time. He ______________ (perform) in public.
6. ________ you ______________ (dance) to a slow song?

Chinese opera

7 **What about you?** Write questions. Work with a partner. Answer each other's questions.

1. go / rock concert ___Have you ever gone to a rock concert?___
2. play / a musical instrument ______
3. take / music lessons ______
4. watch / a band ______
5. listen to / classical music ______
6. sing / in public ______
7. hear / your brother sing ______
8. perform / in public ______

8 **Work in groups of three.** Use words from the list to ask and answer. Take turns.

band	guitar	dance	play
concert	piano	have jazz lessons	sing
drums	saxophone	listen to	take
famous	singer	meet	watch

9 **Listen and repeat.** Then read and write. TR: A23

hip-hop

classical

pop

jazz

rock

1. A large orchestra that includes cellos, violins, a piano, basses, and trumpets often plays ________________ music.
2. Some music uses spoken words instead of singing. It's called ________________.
3. A type of music with swing and rhythm that began 100 years ago and had links to the music of West Africa is ________________.
4. This music is made for many, many people to enjoy. It's easy to listen to. It's ________________ music.
5. We call this music with a strong beat and fast rhythm ________________.

10 **Work with a partner.** Talk and stick. Rank the types of music (1 = most favorite). Discuss your favorite music and give examples of songs and performers.

1	2	3	4	5

GRAMMAR TR: A24

He sings **more loudly than** I do.
I play the guitar **as well as** my brother.
She plays the violin **better than** he does.
He practices piano **less often than** I do.

11 **Read and write.** Make comparisons. Use five words from the list.

beautifully fast hard often slow well worse

1. He's good. He plays guitar ______________ he plays the drums.
2. That's not good. The orchestra sounds ______________ the band.
3. She practices ______________ than he does. She plays at least twice a day.
4. I dance hip-hop ______________ I dance rock.
5. I play the piano ______________ my older sister.

12 **Play a game.** Play with a partner. Take turns. Spin and make sentences with a comparison.

13 **Listen and read.** TR: A25

It's All Music

People made music before they could write about it. The oldest instrument ever found is more than 35,000 years old. It's a flute. Instruments of this type are called wind instruments. Like the sound of the wind, the music comes from moving air. Some wind instruments have a special piece for your mouth. The piece also helps to make the sound. Each instrument has a shape that makes its sound different. Some wind instruments have holes for fingers. Others have buttons to press. Holes and buttons let you change the way the air travels to change the melody.

Another way to make music is with strings. When you slide a finger over a string or pluck it, it makes music. Most string instruments have thick or thin strings and long or short strings to make different notes.

The shape of the body of a stringed instrument also helps to make the sound. Musicians use a bow to play some string instruments. The bow is a piece of wood with hairs or a string stretched between its ends.

You can also make music by hitting or shaking something that makes a sound. Percussion instruments can be made from many things. That's because most things make a sound when you hit them. An empty space inside the instrument makes the sound louder. Percussion instruments with strings make music when the strings are hit. A drum is a percussion instrument. A piano is a percussion instrument, too. When piano keys are pressed, hammers inside the piano hit the strings to make music.

Woman playing guzheng, Xi'an, China

14 Choose the best answer.

1. A drum is a __________.

   a. string instrument b. percussion instrument c. wind instrument

2. If you press a key on a wind instrument, the sound changes because __________.

   a. your finger is heavy

   b. it holds the instrument tightly

   c. the path for the air changes

3. An empty space inside percussion instruments makes the sound __________.

   a. softer b. faster c. louder

4. Some string instruments are played with a __________.

   a. bow b. hammer c. key

15 **Match the instruments and their types.** Work with a partner. Check the correct column.

	Wind	String	Percussion
Drums			
Flute			
Guitar			
Piano			
Saxophone			
Violin			

weird but true

Mozart composed his first song when he was four years old.

16 **Work in groups of three.** Invent a unique band that mixes different musical instruments. What six instruments would you choose?

Paragraphs of Contrast

Paragraphs of contrast show the differences between things. You can use facts and descriptive details to contrast different characteristics. You can also use words like *but, although, unlike, while, instead,* and *in contrast* to show things are not the same.

17 **Read.** Read the paragraphs about two ways to compose music. How does the writer show they are different? Underline the words used.

Composing, Then and Now

In the past, composers traditionally created their music with paper and pen. But now, technology — such as computer and phone apps — is changing how music is made. Although some composers still write by hand, more and more are using these new tools. Before, a composer would write notes on lined measures of music. In contrast, apps let the composer hum a melody, and then the apps write the musical notes!

Many people think that composing music was more difficult in the past. When composers wanted to make changes as they wrote, they had to stop and erase notes. It was a messy, slow process. Some new apps, unlike old erasers, make correction easy. These apps can show music as a moving stream of color. To make changes, the composer can pull and twist music with his or her fingers on the screen. While a traditional composer is busy cleaning ink off fingers, a modern composer can write more songs instead!

18 **Write.** Write about two styles of music or two musical instruments. How are they different? Use words and expressions that show contrast.

19 **Work in a small group.** Share your writing.

NATIONAL GEOGRAPHIC

Mission

Change through music.

- Work with a partner. How does music change how you think and feel? How can music make the world a better place?
- Choose a song that changed how you think. Write some words of the song in the box.

- Discuss how and why the song changed you.

"Music can change the world. It can inspire people to care, to do something positive, to make a difference."

Jack Johnson

National Geographic Arts Ambassador for the Environment

20 Make an instrument.

1. Work in small groups and research homemade musical instruments.
2. Collect trash and junk, and make a musical instrument.
3. Join other groups with instruments and practice.
4. Have a concert!

Now I can . . .

- ○ identify musical instruments.
- ○ talk about musical styles.
- ○ express preferences.
- ○ write a paragraph of contrast.

Unit 4

Life Out There

In this unit, I will . . .

- discuss life in space.
- discuss space exploration.
- express my opinion.
- write a persuasive paragraph.

Circle the correct letter.

1. What are they looking at?

   a. the clouds b. the stars

2. What time of the day is it?

   a. late afternoon b. the middle of the night

3. Why are they wearing coats?

   a. They are on the moon. b. It's cold.

The Milky Way

2 Listen and repeat. TR: A31

Earth is a **planet** that moves around the sun. Other planets also **orbit** the sun. The sun and planets make up our **solar system.** The sun is a star like the stars you see in the sky at night. Some stars have solar systems with planets, too. There may be another planet out there that has an **atmosphere** with oxygen to breathe.

A star and the planets that orbit around it make up a solar system. Stars and solar systems make up a **galaxy.** Our galaxy is the Milky Way. It has about 100 billion stars. Outside our galaxy, there are more galaxies! There are more galaxies in the **universe** than there are stars in a galaxy. How many? We don't know! There are too many, and many are too far away to see.

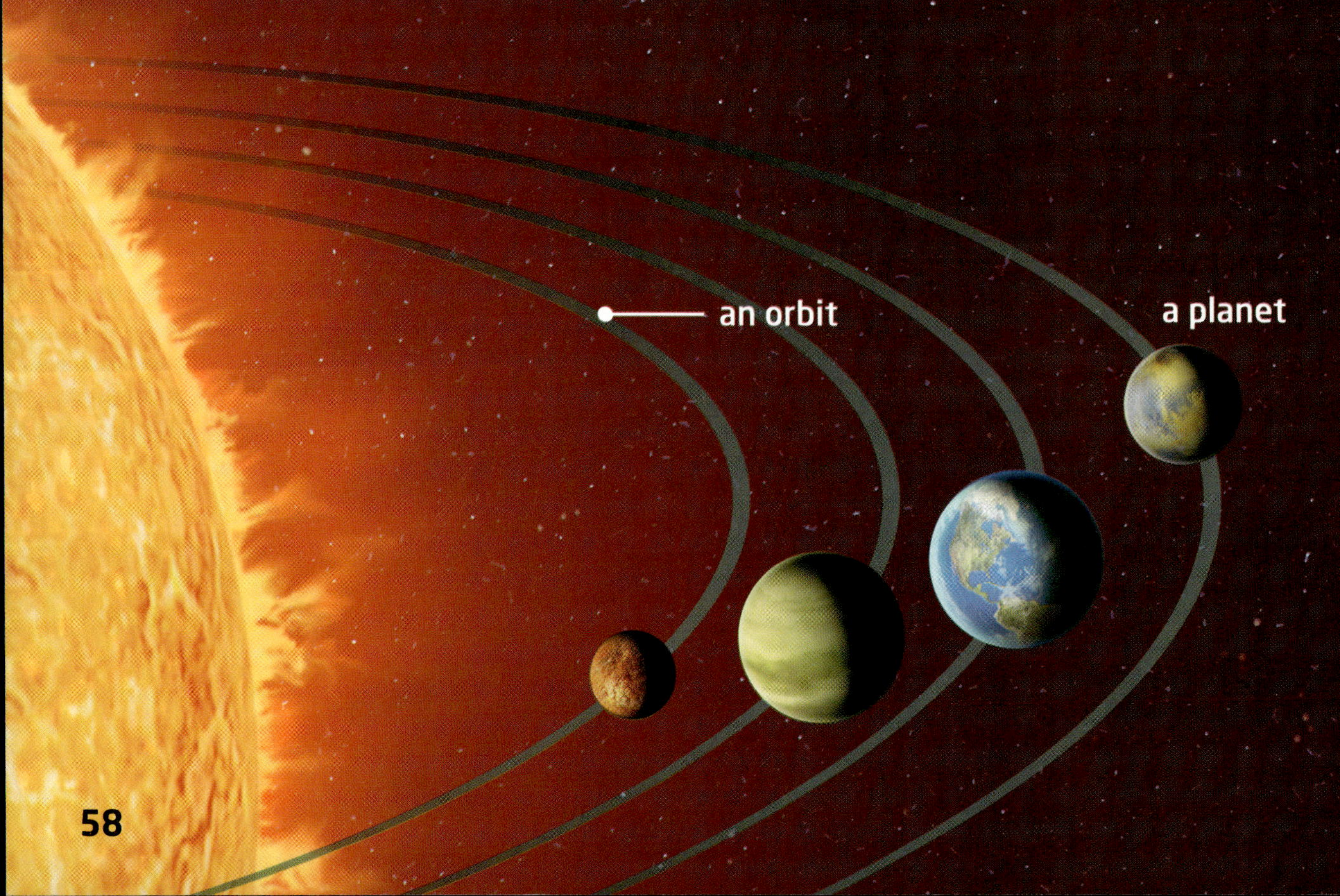

A **comet** is a cloud of rock, ice, and gas that orbits the sun. Many earth years pass in its **journey** around the sun. Scientists keep **data** on comets to know when they will appear.

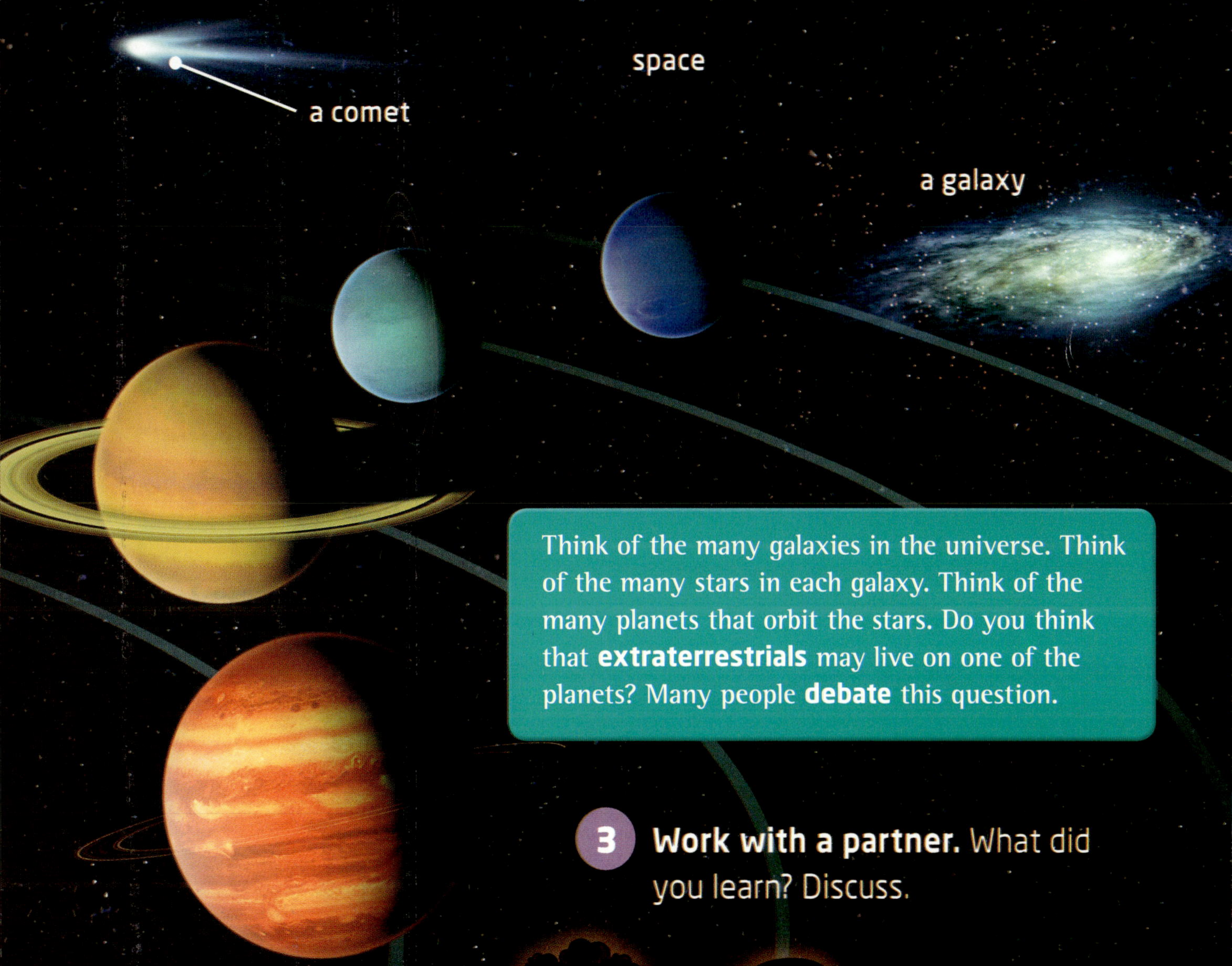

Think of the many galaxies in the universe. Think of the many stars in each galaxy. Think of the many planets that orbit the stars. Do you think that **extraterrestrials** may live on one of the planets? Many people **debate** this question.

3 **Work with a partner.** What did you learn? Discuss.

4 Listen, read, and sing. TR: A32

Deep in Outer Space

Let's all take a journey
past the atmosphere,
beyond our solar system,
far away from here.

We might find a new planet.
We might find a new place.
We might find things we've never seen
deep in outer space.

Deep in outer space,
who knows what we might find?
Deep in outer space,
deep in outer space!

Somewhere in the universe
we might find a moon
where flowers grow.
You never know,
but I wish we'd get there soon!

CHORUS

But right here on planet Earth
life is all around.
Our world is full of color,
texture, light, and sound.

We can take a journey
right outside our door
and see the wonder of life on Earth
and so much more!

CHORUS

Deep in outer space.

5 **Work with a partner.** Talk about life in outer space. Take turns.

- moon
- planet
- solar system
- universe

Rosette Nebula

GRAMMAR TR: A33

If a planet has an atmosphere, it **may** have life.
There **might** be life on other planets.

Do you think astronauts **might** go to the moon again?
Yes, but it **may** be very simple life.

6 **Read.** Check the true sentences.

1. Some stars may have planets like Earth. ☐
2. We may find extraterrestrials on a distant planet. ☐
3. A meteor might hit Earth. ☐
4. The Milky Way might be a galaxy. ☐
5. Earth may have an atmosphere. ☐
6. You may become an astronaut. ☐

7 Complete the sentences.

are	is	live
may be	may discover	may live

1. There ____________________ oxygen in planets in other galaxies.
2. There ____________________ no oxygen on the moon.
3. Extraterrestrials ____________________ on other planets.
4. Astronauts ____________________ in the space station for some time.
5. There ____________________ other solar systems in the universe.
6. One day, scientists ____________________ life on other planets.

8 **What do you think?** Write sentences.

1. green skin/extraterrestrial Extraterrestrials might not have green skin like they do in the movies.

2. comet/lifetime ______________________

3. universe/galaxies ______________________

4. comet/our planet ______________________

5. find/life ______________________

9 **Work in groups of three.** Take turns. Make a sentence about life in the universe. Your partners will add more information.

10 **Listen and repeat.** Then read and write. **TR: A34**

a space station

SETI: **Search** for ExtraTerrestrial Intelligence

1. A powerful ____________________ is needed to send anything into space.
2. People live and work in the ____________________. They perform experiments in space.
3. Extraterrestrials probably would not speak English. It would be difficult to ____________________ with them.
4. I saw a documentary about the ____________________ for life in other galaxies.
5. Someday we may land a ____________________ on the moon again.
6. Anyone who travels through space is an ____________________.

11 **Listen and stick.** Work with a partner. Take turns describing the rocket liftoff. **TR: A35**

1	2	3	4	5

GRAMMAR TR: A36

Did **everyone** see that comet?
Someone will go to Mars one day.

Does **anyone** want to be an astronaut?
No one can see all the stars in the universe.

12 **Read and write.** Complete the paragraph.

anyone   everyone   no one   someone

_______________ likes to debate about life on other planets. _______________ knows for sure if there is life out there or not. If _______________ tells you that they know, that person really doesn't know! Are you _______________ who likes to debate? I will debate about life in space with _______________ who wants to. _______________ knows the answer, but _______________ has an opinion!

13 **Work with a partner.** What about you?

1. Does anyone in your family think there is life on other planets?
2. Name one thing everyone in your family does.
3. Name one thing no one in your family believes.
4. Name a funny habit someone in your family has.

14 **Play a game.** Cut out the cards on page 165. Make sentences. Take turns.

15 **Listen and read.** TR: A37

Listening for Life

If extraterrestrials live on other planets, we can't see them. Planets in other solar systems are extremely far away. We can't see the planets, even with our biggest telescopes. But what if the extraterrestrials want to communicate with us? What if they are sending messages? This signal would travel through space. After many years, it might reach our solar system. The signal would be very weak. It would be hidden in the noise from other places in space. We would need special tools to hear it.

Scientists at SETI have made a tool for listening. It uses 42 satellite dishes that are connected together. Scientists plan to have 350 dishes one day. They point all the dishes at the same place in the sky. Then they search for any data they can hear. The dishes can hear very weak signals. For example, they could hear a cell phone on a planet in our solar system. (That's if someone had a cell phone on Jupiter!) The dishes pick up noise from radios on Earth, too. Scientists must be careful to avoid this noise.

We have not heard from an extraterrestrial yet. But is it possible that they are listening to us? If they are, most could not have heard us yet. We have used radios for less than 100 years. That's not much time for the big distances in the universe. In that time, our signal could only reach a small number of stars. Extraterrestrials from nearby solar systems would not hear us for thousands of years.

Length of Time Needed for Radio Waves to Reach Earth

16 Check T for *True* and F for *False*.

1. Extraterrestrials have listened to our radio waves for over 100 years. Ⓣ Ⓕ
2. SETI dishes listen for life by listening for radio signals. Ⓣ Ⓕ
3. Scientists point the SETI dishes in many directions. Ⓣ Ⓕ
4. Radio waves from Earth are a problem for SETI scientists. Ⓣ Ⓕ

17 **Should we search for life?** Write why and why not.

I think it's a good idea to search for life because . . .	I think it's a bad idea to search for life because . . .

18 **Work with a partner.** Look at the chart and discuss. Support your opinion.

weird but true: The first astronauts were fruit flies. They were launched on February 20, 1947.

Paragraphs of Persuasion

In persuasive paragraphs, you write to convince the reader of your opinion. To persuade the reader, you use facts to support your opinion. Write strong sentences that show you believe in what you are saying. Introduce your facts with expressions such as *research shows, according to,* and *the facts show that.*

19 **Read.** How does the writer persuade? Underline the words.

Forever Searching

Long ago, people thought that the sun and planets orbited Earth. We like to think that we are at the center of things. But scientists studied the stars carefully. Their research shows that we are not at the center. Copernicus was the first to say that Earth orbits the sun. He was right. And the sun orbits the center of the galaxy. The universe has many stars that we can't see. And, according to some NASA scientists, somewhere there may be life.

Why do we search? The facts show that we have always been people who search. For example, Zheng was an explorer from China who traveled as far as Arabia and the Horn of Africa in the 1400s. Frederick Cook went to the North Pole in 1908. And Roald Amundsen traveled to the South Pole in 1911. We search both on Earth and in space because we like to find answers. And a big question is, are we alone? We will search until we know.

20 **Write.** Do you think we should search for life in space? Take a position. Think about cost, usefulness, urgent problems on Earth, and so on. Use facts to persuade.

21 **Work in a small group.** Share your writing.

NATIONAL GEOGRAPHIC

Mission

Live curious.

- Think about things you want to know. How can you find answers?
- Work with a partner. Discuss. Do you search for answers even when it's difficult? How do you feel when you finally find the answer? Write your ideas in the box.

"We finally have the tools and technology to answer this age-old question: Are we alone? Jupiter's moon Europa is a beautiful place to go and explore that question."

Kevin Hand

Planetary Scientist/Astrobiologist

Emerging Explorer

- Work with another group. Share your ideas. Are they the same or different? Which idea does everyone like best?

Jupiter

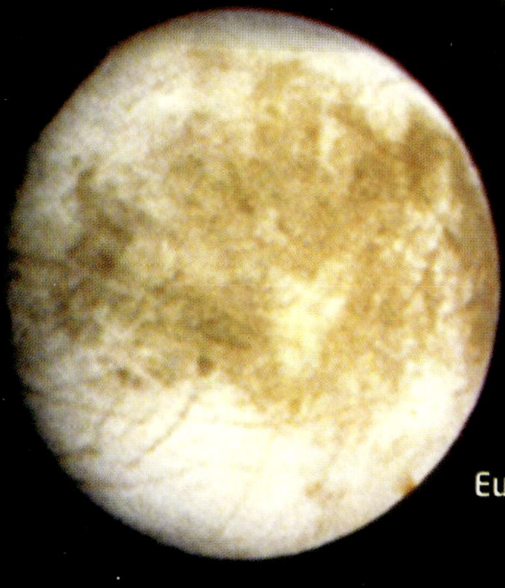

Europa

22 Research and make a model of a type of place where you think we could find life.

1. Choose a type of place you think might have life.
2. Research information.
3. Use the information you find and your imagination to re-create the surface of the type of planet or moon you choose. Use cardboard, paper, and other materials.
4. Draw different life forms as you imagine them.

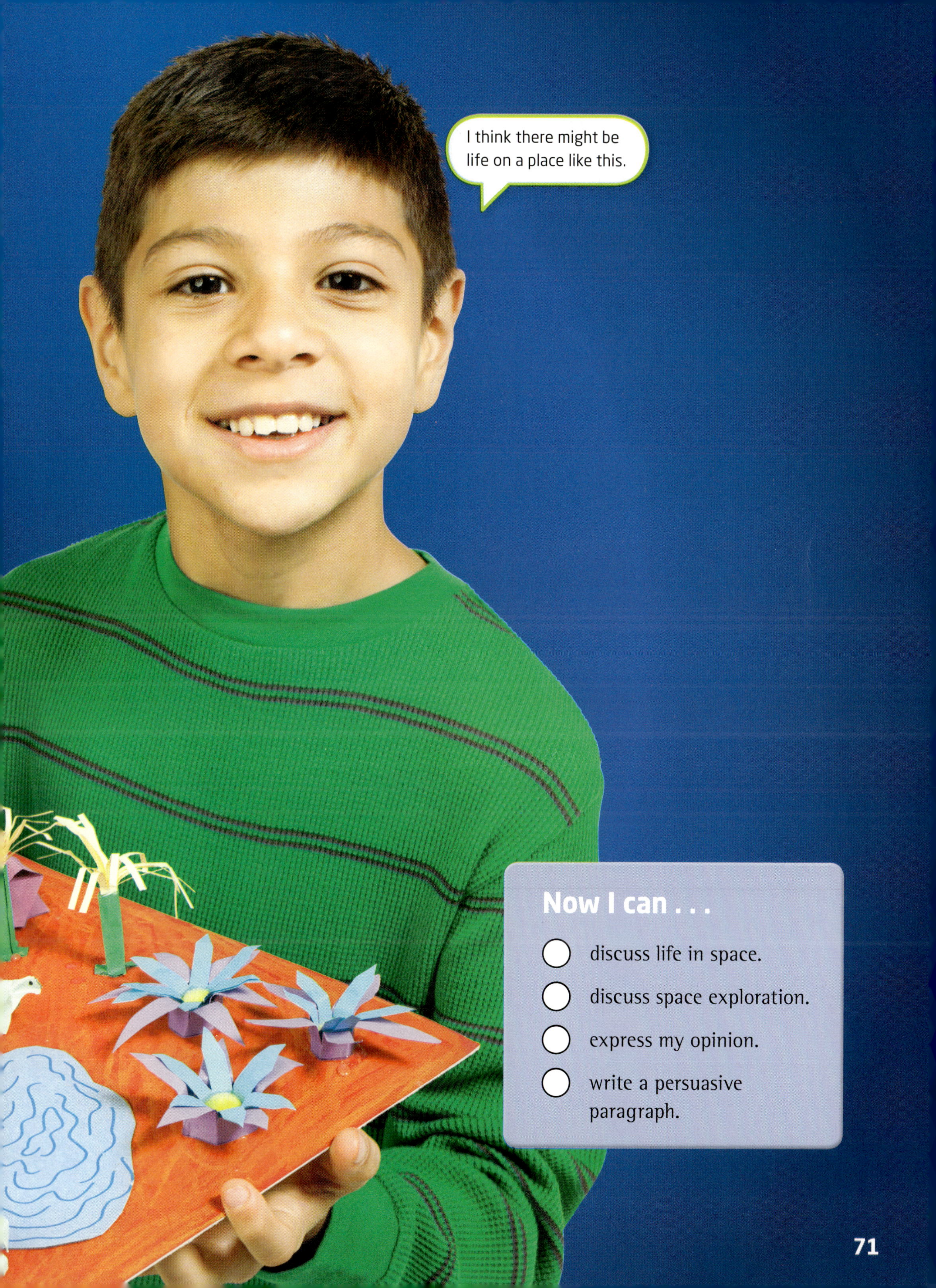

Now I can . . .

- ◯ discuss life in space.
- ◯ discuss space exploration.
- ◯ express my opinion.
- ◯ write a persuasive paragraph.

Unit 5

Arts Lost and Found

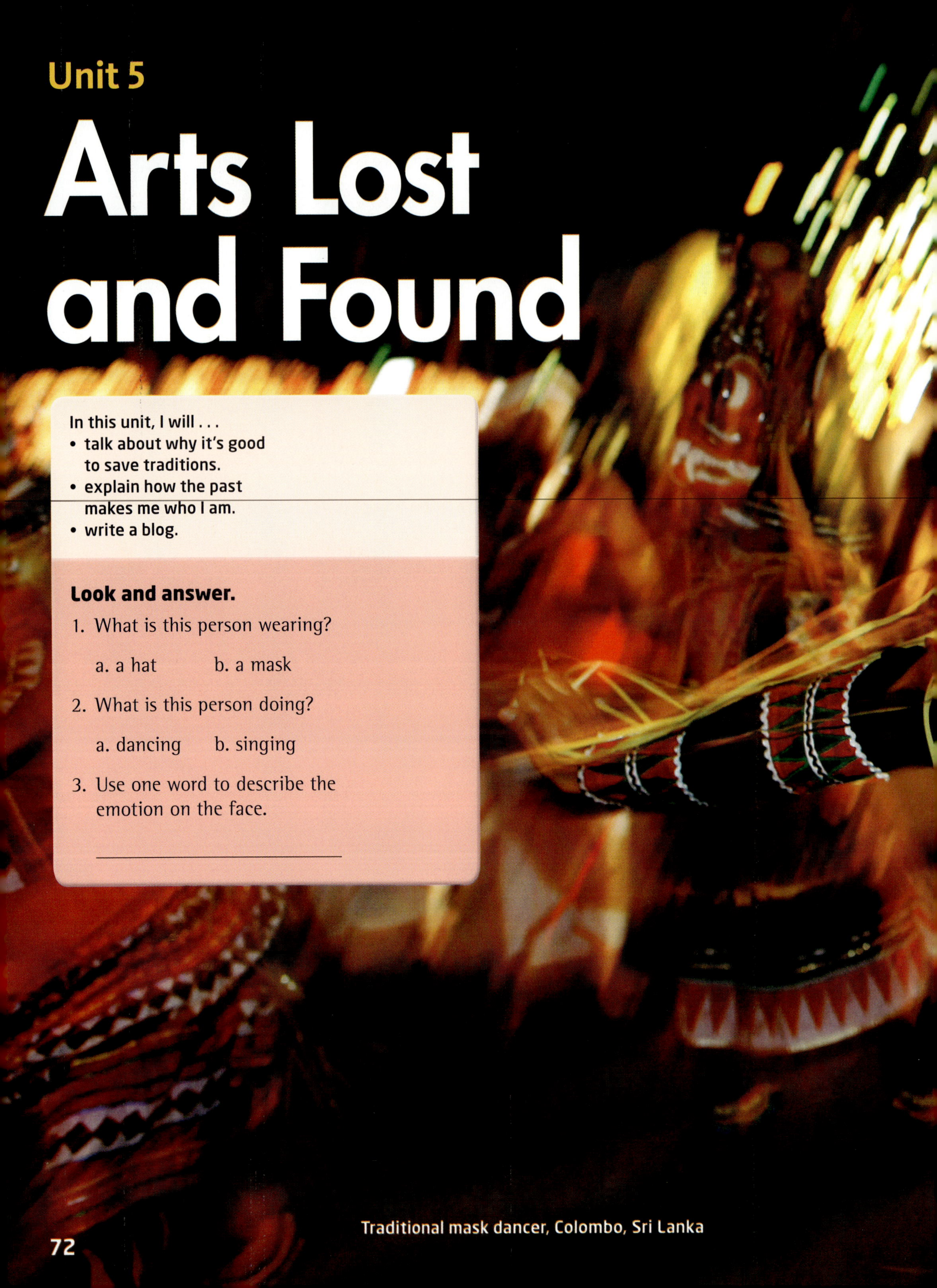

In this unit, I will . . .
- talk about why it's good to save traditions.
- explain how the past makes me who I am.
- write a blog.

Look and answer.

1. What is this person wearing?

   a. a hat b. a mask

2. What is this person doing?

   a. dancing b. singing

3. Use one word to describe the emotion on the face.

   ____

Traditional mask dancer, Colombo, Sri Lanka

1 **Listen and read.** TR: A38

2 **Listen and repeat.** TR: A39

Everyone should be **proud** of who they are. What makes you who you are? Part of who you are comes from the past. It comes from the **culture** of your parents, grandparents, and people before them. It comes from the **language** you speak, the **art** you see, the stories and music you hear, and the **traditions** you **share.**

Dragon boats are a 2000-year-old Chinese tradition. Racers must cooperate and row together to win. Today dragon boat racing has become a modern world sport.

Storytelling isn't always done with words. In Laos, dancers tell stories with their hands. The dances are part of their history. This history is **passed down** from one **generation** to the next.

The people of Tabasco, Mexico, keep their history alive. This **local** boy has clay on his face. He will do the jaguar dance to bring rain. His people speak an old language that came from the Olmec thousands of years ago.

The people of Ghana **hold on** to their tradition of **weaving** beautiful cloth. **Tourists** come to Ghana to buy cloth. The money that the tourists pay helps the **future** of the **community.**

3 Work with a partner. What did you learn? Discuss.

4 Listen, read, and sing. TR: A40

Keep Your Culture Strong

Knowing your history is important.
Holding on to your culture is an excellent thing!
Knowing your history is important.
It's up to you to keep your culture strong!

What special art does your culture bring to our world?
What special thing does your family bring to our world?
Weaving? Learn to do it!
Storytelling? Learn to tell it!
What brings your culture pride?

CHORUS

What special art does your culture bring to our world?
What special thing does your family bring to our world?
Embroidery? Learn to sew it!
Sculpture? Learn to sculpt it!
What brings your culture pride?

Your grandparents may seem old to you,
but they know a thing or two!

CHORUS

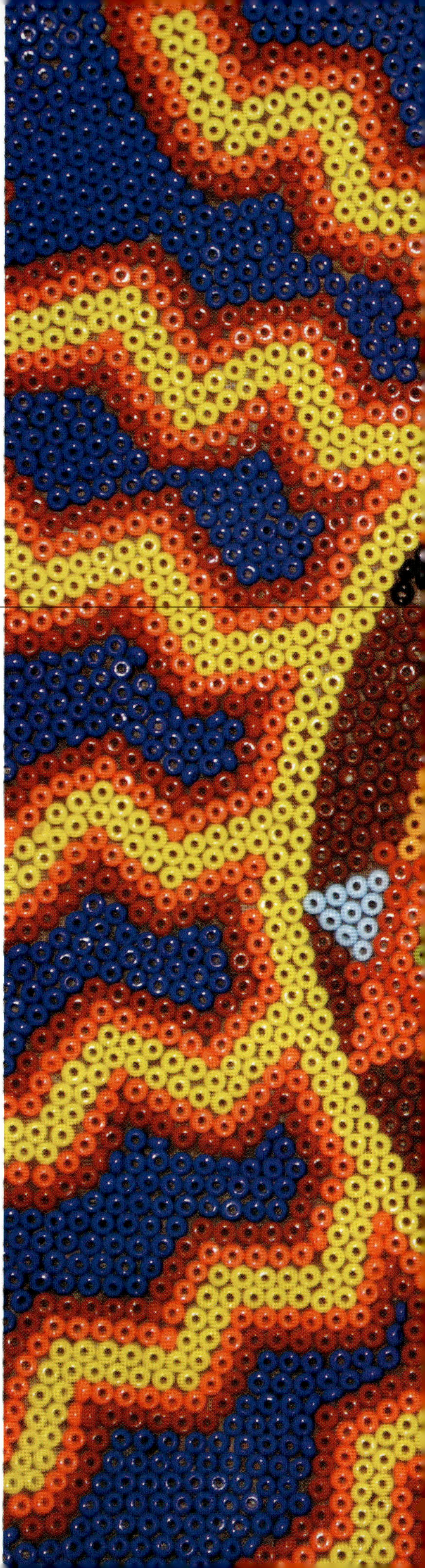

5 Work with a partner. Ask and answer.

1. What special art does your culture bring to our world?
2. What special thing does your family bring to our world?
3. What would you like to learn to do?

GRAMMAR TR: A41

Knowing your history is important.
Holding on to your traditions is a good thing.
Passing down family stories connects generations.
Creating art is a good way to share your culture.

6 **Read.** Complete the sentences.

cook make paint row share weave

1. ______________ a boat is hard to do with another person.
2. ______________ cloth was my grandmother's work.
3. ______________ art is exciting!
4. ______________ your traditions helps other people understand you.
5. ______________ on wood is fun for people who like colors.
6. ______________ traditional recipes is another way to keep your culture alive.

7 **What about you?** Complete the sentences about you and your family.

1. Painting is my father's hobby.
2. Teaching ______________.
3. Cooking ______________.
4. Helping ______________.
5. Taking photos ______________.
6. Reading ______________.

8 Complete the conversation.

Mario: Grandpa, did you **listen to music** when you were a kid?

Grandpa: Yes, I did. ______________________ was one of my favorite hobbies!

Mario: And did you **go to the movies?**

Grandpa: Of course! I went every Sunday. ______________________ was the most important event of the weekend!

Mario: Did you **talk** to your friends **on the phone?**

Grandpa: No, I didn't. ______________________ was very expensive when I was a kid!

Mario: And did you **play sports?**

Grandpa: Not much. My parents thought that ______________________ was a waste of time. They wanted me to study all the time! But I still played soccer with my friends!

Mario: How about chores? Did you **help around the house?**

Grandpa: Of course! ______________________ was something everyone had to do!

9 Work in groups of three. Take turns. Express your opinion.

listening to stories	making art	saving traditions	visiting family
watching dancers	singing traditional songs	looking at old photos	

10 **Listen and repeat.**
Then read and write. TR: A42

handcrafted

sculpture

embroidery

pottery

jewelry making

1. When a work of art is made by hand, we say it's ______________________.
2. People use ______________________ to make their clothes more beautiful and decorative.
3. ______________________ is made from clay that dries and becomes hard. Sometimes it is heated in an oven.
4. To make a ______________________, artists can use materials such as wood, stone, metal, or ice.
5. ______________________ is popular. Most kids like to make bracelets.

11 **Look, rank (1 = most favorite), and stick.** Work with a partner. Discuss your preferences.

1	2	3	4	5

GRAMMAR TR: A43

My friends are good at **making** jewelry.
I like **eating** traditional foods.
My mother enjoys **embroidering** clothes.
I'm interested in **learning** about new places.

12 **Read and complete the sentences.** Use the words from the list.

cooperating making passing sharing storytelling traveling

1. Young people today are very interested in ________________ their traditions.
2. I'm very excited about ________________ to the country of my grandparents.
3. Do you like ________________? Storytellers like ________________ down their traditions.
4. I enjoy ________________ traditional jewelry.
5. We can save our rich history by ________________ with people from traditional communities.

13 **Play a game.** Cut out the cube on page 167. Work with a partner. Take turns making sentences.

14 Listen and read. TR: A44

Modern Music with Ancient Roots

Did you know that modern music comes from traditional music? Every generation changes the music of the past. They make it their own. Reggae music began in Jamaica, but it has its roots in African music. Africans came to Jamaica and brought their music. It mixed with music from Europe. Now, reggae impacts music all over the world. Dancehall and hip-hop music came from reggae!

Shaabi music is based on Egyptian folk music. It is played with the saxophone and electronic keyboard, which are modern instruments. But it is also played with a kanun, a traditional string instrument. The instruments are different, but the musical roots are the same!

Norteño is a modern type of Mexican music with folk roots. Old Norteño music was played with an accordion and a Mexican guitar. Then Norteño bands heard rock music. They added drums, saxophones, and electronic keyboards to their bands! Modern Norteño has a stronger beat than the traditional music.

In Japan, many people listen to J-pop music. J-pop is the name for all modern Japanese pop music. It includes many modern music types and instruments like electric guitars and keyboards. In the 1920s, when Japanese pop music began, performers used harmonicas and string instruments. The music combined Western jazz and soul with a traditional style of Japanese singing. Today every J-pop artist or band selects and combines the instruments and music rhythms they like best with their Japanese-language songs.

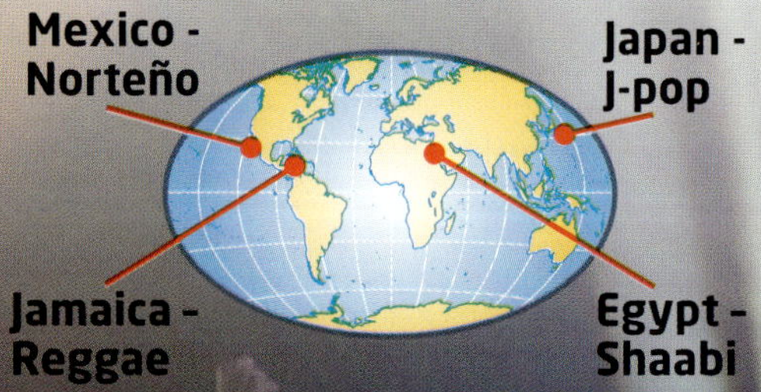

15 Read and write.

1. Where did reggae music begin? ______________________
2. In what country is Norteño performed? ______________________
3. What kind of music influenced J-pop? ______________________
4. Which music is based on Egyptian folk music? ______________________
5. Which music influenced dancehall and hip-hop? ______________________

16 **Compare the music.** Work with a partner.

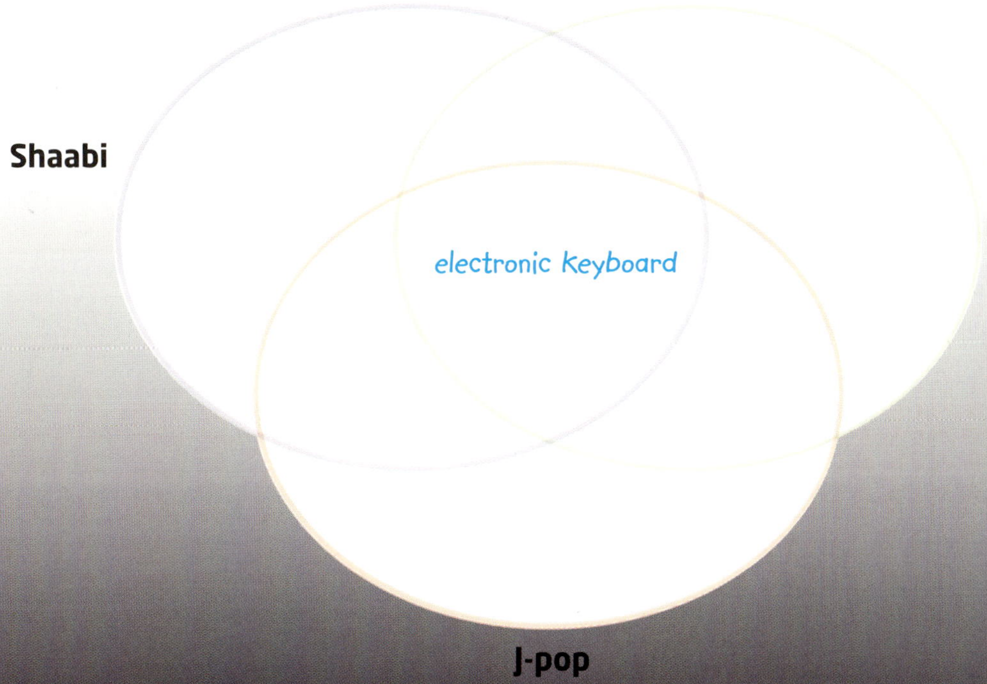

weird but true

Mice sing to each other at night.

17 **Work with a partner.** Make new music. Invent a new musical style. It can be completely new, or you can modernize a style you know. What styles would you mix? What instruments would you use?

Blog Entries

In a personal blog, you write about your thoughts. You describe what you saw, heard, or felt. A blog sounds like an informal conversation. You can ask your readers to post a response on your blog. You can use expressions like *so cool, awesome, hated it,* and *laugh out loud (lol).*

18 **Read.** What informal expressions does the writer use in her blog? Underline them.

« » Cecilia's Blog

The coolest vacation ever!!!

My family and I went to Machu Picchu in Peru. It was awesome. First, I took a long train ride with my family to Aguas Calientes. From there we took a bus to Machu Picchu. The bus went slowly up the steep mountain. (I'm really glad the bus was slow.) LOL. From the bus window I saw llamas eating grass.

When we arrived, I was excited. It was so cool to see the ruins. The Incas who built Machu Picchu were great architects. My family and I climbed the stairs all the way up to the Sun Gate. It was a steep climb. We stopped to rest a few times because I was incredibly tired. At the top, it was wonderful. We could see everything! I think my photos are fabulous. Tell me what you think.

19 **Write.** Write a blog entry about a family vacation or a special day. Describe your thoughts and feelings.

20 **Work in a group.** Share your writing. Listen and take notes.

NATIONAL GEOGRAPHIC

Mission

Value your cultural traditions.

- Work with a partner. What local culture and traditions are in danger?
- Why should we keep our culture and traditions alive? List some ideas in the box.

"I'm committed to protecting the cultures of the world in hopes that the wisdom of their elders is remembered."

Elizabeth Kapu'uwailani Lindsey
Filmmaker/Anthropologist
National Geographic Fellow

- Work with another group. Share your ideas. Are they the same or different? Which ideas does everyone like best?

21 Make a time capsule of things that show your culture.

1. Work in small groups.
2. Talk about things that show your culture.
3. Choose the best things to include.
4. Put objects in your time capsule.

Now I can . . .

- ◯ talk about why it's good to save traditions.
- ◯ explain how the past makes me who I am.
- ◯ write a blog.

Irregular Verbs

Infinitive	Simple Past	Past Participle	Infinitive	Simple Past	Past Participle
be	was/were	been	light	lit	lit
beat	beat	beaten	lose	lost	lost
become	became	become	make	made	made
begin	began	begun	meet	met	met
bend	bent	bent	pay	paid	paid
bite	bit	bitten	put	put	put
bleed	bled	bled	read	read	read
blow	blew	blown	ride	rode	ridden
break	broke	broken	ring	rang	rung
bring	brought	brought	rise	rose	risen
build	built	built	run	ran	run
buy	bought	bought	say	said	said
catch	caught	caught	see	saw	seen
choose	chose	chosen	sell	sold	sold
come	came	come	send	sent	sent
cost	cost	cost	set	set	set
cut	cut	cut	sew	sewed	sewn
dig	dug	dug	shake	shook	shaken
do	did	done	shine	shone	shone
draw	drew	drawn	show	showed	shown
drink	drank	drunk	shut	shut	shut
drive	drove	driven	sing	sang	sung
eat	ate	eaten	sink	sank	sunk
fall	fell	fallen	sit	sat	sat
feed	fed	fed	sleep	slept	slept
feel	felt	felt	slide	slid	slid
fight	fought	fought	speak	spoke	spoken
find	found	found	spend	spent	spent
fly	flew	flown	spin	spun	spun
forget	forgot	forgotten	stand	stood	stood
forgive	forgave	forgiven	steal	stole	stolen
freeze	froze	frozen	stick	stuck	stuck
get	got	gotten	sting	stung	stung
give	gave	given	stink	stank	stunk
go	went	gone	sweep	swept	swept
grow	grew	grown	swim	swam	swum
hang	hung	hung	swing	swung	swung
have	had	had	take	took	taken
hear	heard	heard	teach	taught	taught
hide	hid	hidden	tear	tore	torn
hit	hit	hit	tell	told	told
hold	held	held	think	thought	thought
hurt	hurt	hurt	throw	threw	thrown
keep	kept	kept	understand	understood	understood
know	knew	known	wake up	woke up	woken up
leave	left	left	wear	wore	worn
lend	lent	lent	win	won	won
let	let	let	write	wrote	written
lie	lay	lain			

isn't it?	**is it?**	**aren't they?**	**are they?**
don't they?	**do they?**	**doesn't it?**	**does it?**
were they?	**weren't they?**	**did it?**	**didn't it?**

anyone	**everyone**	**no one**	**someone**

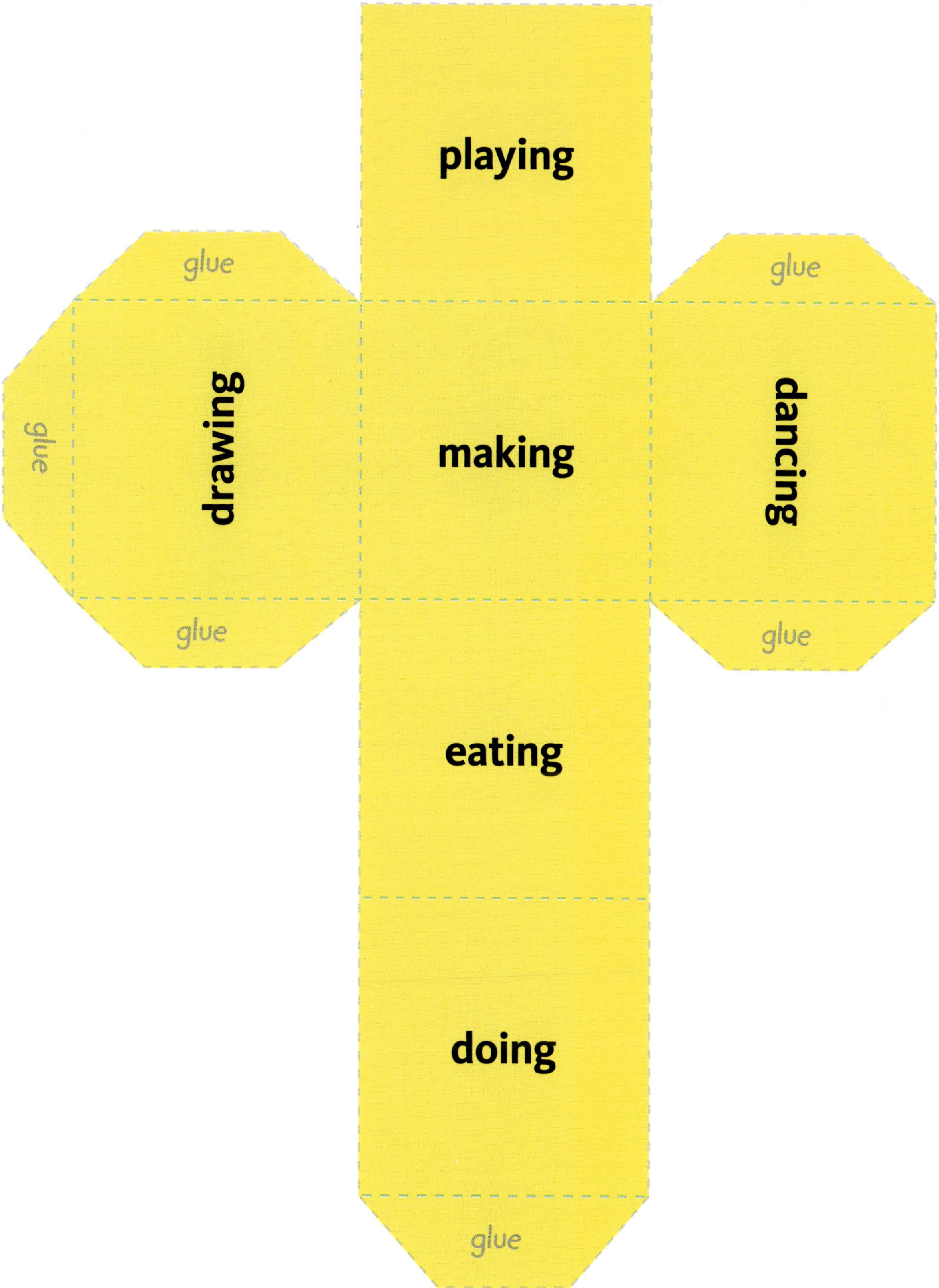
playing
glue
glue
glue
drawing
making
dancing
glue
glue
eating
doing
glue

Our World 5A Workbook

Series Editors
JoAnn (Jodi) Crandall
Joan Kang Shin

Author
Ronald Scro

Unit 1 Extreme Weather 2
Unit 2 Copycat Animals 14
Unit 3 Music in Our World 26
Unit 4 Life Out There 42
Unit 5 Arts Lost and Found 54

Additional Activities 122

National Geographic Learning | Cengage Learning

Australia • Brazil • Japan • Korea • Mexico • Singapore • Spain • United Kingdom • United States

Unit 1

Extreme Weather

1 **Read and write.** Do the Extreme Puzzle!

Across

3. Bad storm with very fast, dangerous winds
8. Go up
11. How fast?
12. Too little rain
13. Go down
15. Storm with strong twisting winds

Down

1. Loud noise from a storm
2. Can make night look like day
4. From low to high or high to low
5. Snow falling hard
6. What you see on the first page of unit 1 in your Student Book (two words)
7. Strong winds blowing in a desert
9. Hot for many days (two words)
10. A storm with fast winds
14. Too much water

2 **Listen and circle.** Listen for the puzzle words. Circle them on the puzzle in Activity 1. **TR: 02**

3 **Unscramble the words.**

1. egnar ________________
2. orpd ________________
3. ughdrot ________________
4. natdoor ________________
5. dazilbrz ________________
6. tansmords ________________

4 **Read and write.** Use the words from Activity 3 to complete the sentences.

1. The water in the lake was low because of the ________________.
2. The winds from the ________________ lifted a car and moved it 30 meters (98 feet)!
3. If there is a ________________ in the temperature, I will need to wear a coat.
4. When it is windy in a desert, there can be a ________________.
5. What was the ________________ of temperatures today, from lowest to highest?
6. In a really bad ________________, sometimes all you can see is white!

5 **Listen and write.** Use verses from the song. **TR: 03**

There's bad weather on the way!
There's bad weather on the way.

Is it going to storm? Yes, it is!
Is there going to be lightning? Yes, there is!
Is there going to be thunder? Yes, there is!

When there's going to be a storm,
I hurry inside!

Be prepared for emergencies.
It's always good to be safe. You'll see!
Grab supplies and a flashlight, too.
Seek shelter. It's the safe thing to do!

Is it going to storm?

Yes, it is!

____

____

____

____

____

____

____

____

____

____

____

____

____

6 **Write a new verse for the song.**

Is/Are ______________________? Yes, ______________!

Is/Are ______________________? Yes, ______________!

Is/Are ______________________? Oh, yes ______________!

GRAMMAR

Is it **going to** be sunny tomorrow? No, it**'s going to** rain.

He**'s going to** stay home because of the storm.

I**'m going to** wear rain boots! They say it**'s going to** rain a lot!

7 **Write.** What are they going to do on a rainy Saturday?

1. Mario / walk / in the rain Mario's going to walk in the rain.
2. Pedro / read / newspaper ________________
3. I / write / story ________________
4. Marta and Carla / listen / radio ________________
5. Pablo / sleep ________________

8 **Answer the questions using the given word.**

1. What's the weather going to be like tomorrow? (ice storm)

   Tomorrow there's going to be an ice storm.
2. What's going to happen if it rains for another day? (flood)

   ____
3. What are you going to do when there is a drought? (water)

   ____
4. When she sees lightning, what is she going to hear soon after? (thunder)

   ____
5. It's going to snow. What is he going to do? (boots)

   ____

9 Read and check.

What is it?	a plan	a shelter	an emergency
1. A hurricane arrives, and the streets are flooding.			
2. The winds are strong, and trees are falling.			
3. Get fresh water and other supplies.			
4. A room under a house. You can go there if there is a hurricane.			
5. Have a radio nearby at all times.			

10 **Complete the sentences.** Use words from the box. Some words may be used more than once.

emergency evacuate flashlight plan shelter supplies

1. I'm going to take this flashlight with me to a(n) shelter.
2. You need a(n) ________ so that you know when to ________.
3. In a(n) ________, you will need ________ like food and water.
4. This is a(n) ________, and everyone must ________ to a(n) ________.
5. My ________ is to keep a(n) ________ with my ________.

11 Read and match.

1. very, very cold
2. winds that spin
3. very hot for a long time
4. hot, dry, and very windy
5. very hot and dry for a long time
6. loud noise

a. drought
b. thunder
c. ice storm
d. sandstorm
e. tornado
f. heat wave

12 Write the temperature change.

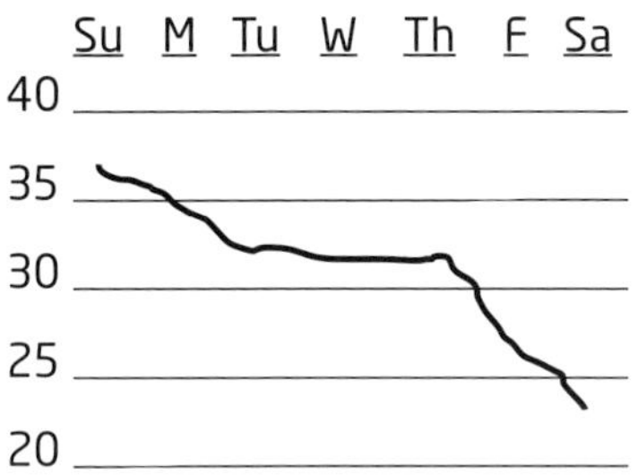

1. a ________ in temperature

2. a ________ in temperature

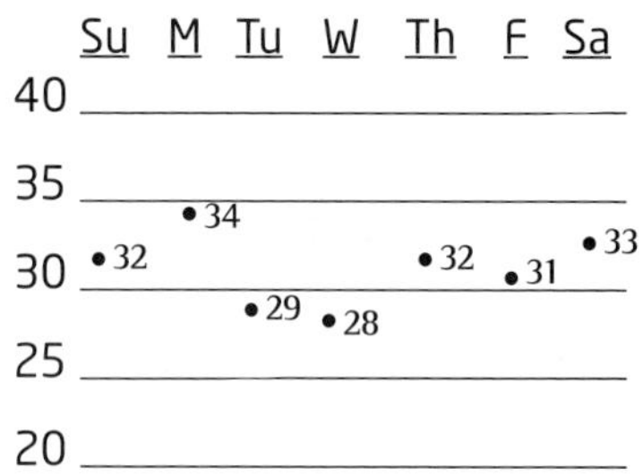

3. a ________ of temperatures

13 Write true sentences.

1. After you see thunder, you may hear lightning.

   After you hear thunder, you may see lightning.

2. A lot of rain after a flood can cause a drought.

   ____

3. It can be very hot during a blizzard or an ice storm.

   ____

4. The wind speed is slow in a tropical storm.

   ____

14 **Work with a partner.** Student 1, go to page 122. Student 2, go to page 124.

GRAMMAR

If					
If	I	**give** you a pen,	(then)	you	**can** write sentences.
	the weather	**is** bad,		I	**stay** home.
	there	**is** a snow storm,		school	**closes** early.
	we	**forget** an umbrella,		it	always **rains**.

School closes early if there is a snow storm.
It always rains if I forget an umbrella.

15 Write what you see.

1. If she sees a stop sign, she stops her bike ______________________.

2. If he sees that it is raining, ______________ ______________________.

3. ______________________ ______________________, we stand at the bus stop.

4. ______________________ ______________________ ______________________.

5. ______________________ ______________________ ______________________.

6. ______________________ ______________________ ______________________.

16 **Listen.** Check **T** for *True* and **F** for *False*. **TR: 04**

1. If a hurricane is coming, Xavier goes to visit his aunt. Ⓣ Ⓕ
2. Xavier puts on his winter coat if it snows. Ⓣ Ⓕ
3. If a storm is coming, Berta listens to the radio. Ⓣ Ⓕ
4. If it snows, Berta watches TV. Ⓣ Ⓕ

17 **Write what the weather is going to be like.** Then explain what you normally do in that weather.

1. 

It's going to rain. If it rains,

I always stay home.

2. 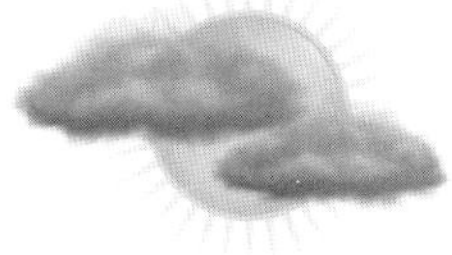

____

____

3. 

____

____

4. 

____

____

18 **Read and match.**

1. If there is lightning,
2. If the temperature drops and rises,
3. If a tropical storm comes,
4. If the wind speed is 120 kilometers per hour (74 miles),
5. If it's hot for two weeks,
6. If an ice storm comes,

a. the temperature drops.
b. it is a heat wave.
c. there is also thunder.
d. it is a hurricane.
e. there is a range of temperatures.
f. it will bring rain and high winds.

19 **Listen and read.** TR: 05

Weather Change

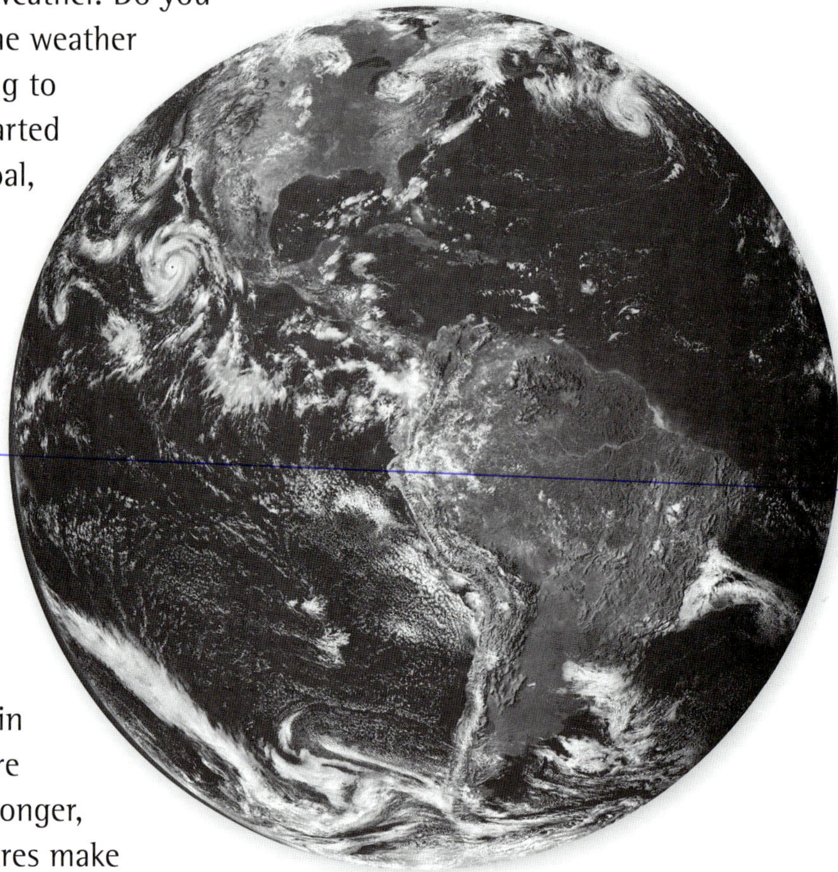

We've always had extreme weather. Do you know that there is more extreme weather now than in the past? According to many scientists, this change started when people started to burn coal, oil, and gas.

The average temperature on Earth is rising. Some droughts are longer and hotter. More of the ice on mountains melts faster. If this water goes to the sea, the sea level rises.

Different places have different changes in the weather. Some places have less rain. Other places have more rain and floods. In most places, there are more storms. Storms are stronger, too. The warmer sea temperatures make hurricanes stronger.

Weather change is a fact. But we can do something. For example, we can make factories and cars more efficient. That way, we can burn less coal, oil, and gas. We can also build stronger houses in safer areas. We can use less energy.

There are also some practical things that everyone can do to be prepared for more extreme weather. People should have a plan and supplies for emergencies. People who live in areas that can flood or in hurricane areas should evacuate in an emergency.

weird but true

The coldest temperature ever recorded on Earth was −89.2°C (−129°F) at Vostok, Antarctica, on July 21, 1983.

20 Circle the best answer.

1. When the weather gets warmer,
   a. ice on mountains melts faster.
   b. the seas rise.
   c. both a and b.
2. To slow weather change, we can
   a. build stronger houses.
   b. burn less coal, oil, and gas.
   c. both a and b.
3. Hurricanes are stronger because
   a. the sea water is warmer.
   b. droughts are longer and hotter.
   c. people don't evacuate.

21 **Work with a partner.** Write what you learned from the text.

What did you know?

What did you learn?

What do you want to know?

22 **Read *Safe not Sorry!* on page 16 of your Student Book.**

How did the writer plan her writing? Read the steps.

1. The writer chose something that happened.
2. Next, the writer wrote things that happened in the order they happened.
3. Then the writer wrote about her feelings about the things that happened.

Feelings
Scary, but a little exciting, too
Everyone was worried.
I am so happy we covered the windows.

4. Next, the writer added descriptions of how she lived the experience through her senses. In the chart below, see the sense words used. Notice that the writer didn't tell about all her senses. You can tell about all or only some senses.

See	Hear	Touch	Taste	Smell
part of a tree	weather forecaster	heavy wood		
wood on the window	strong winds			
	hard rain			
	loud noise			

5. Next, the writer wrote a first sentence to say what the paragraph was about. *Last year, the weather forecaster told us that a hurricane was coming.*
6. Then the writer wrote what happened in order. She included information about what she saw, what she heard, and how she felt.
7. Finally, the writer wrote a sentence to close the paragraph. *Next time, I won't say the wood is too heavy.*

23 **Plan to write about your extreme weather experience.** Answer the questions and complete the chart.

1. What extreme weather experience will you write about?

___

2. What feelings will you write about?

___

See	Hear	Touch	Taste	Smell

24 **Follow the steps on page 12.** In your notebook, write your paragraph about an extreme weather experience.

25 **Express yourself.** Plan to write about something that happened to you. Choose one of the items below. Then complete the table.

☐ a happy thing ☐ a scary thing ☐ a beautiful thing

What experience will you describe?	What words will you use to describe your senses?	What words will you use to describe your feelings?

26 **Write each thing that happened.** Put the events in order.

1. ___
2. ___
3. ___

27 **Write your personal narrative in your notebook.**

Unit 2

Copycat Animals

1 **Find and circle.** Hidden words are down and across.

W	F	G	Q	I	N	S	E	C	T	U	L	H	X	L
M	R	E	O	F	E	N	A	H	E	C	U	U	I	R
C	O	P	I	E	S	J	Z	A	N	P	O	N	O	F
A	D	W	A	F	P	A	P	R	E	D	A	T	O	R
M	I	D	G	Q	E	N	I	A	N	G	W	T	Y	I
O	H	B	H	I	C	S	U	C	E	B	O	J	V	G
U	B	O	I	M	I	T	A	T	E	S	Y	I	X	H
F	V	Q	D	I	E	S	K	E	R	P	O	B	O	T
L	S	R	E	C	S	M	U	R	P	O	L	K	R	E
A	T	K	A	P	U	E	J	I	E	T	K	U	H	N
G	O	S	T	R	I	P	E	S	O	S	I	T	P	A
E	C	D	X	E	I	J	R	T	U	A	V	T	E	Z
D	M	Q	S	Y	X	P	O	I	S	O	N	O	U	S
A	F	M	R	O	O	U	P	C	A	C	Y	I	Z	U
Z	A	M	H	E	C	R	E	S	E	M	B	L	E	X

resemble	copies
frighten	hunt
poisonous	prey
predator	insect
imitates	stripes
species	spots
camouflage	hide
characteristics	

2 **Read and write.** Use words from the puzzle.

1. It's hard to see some animals because of the marks on their bodies.

   The ________________ on some animals can be used as ________________.

2. A/An ________________ uses camouflage so it doesn't frighten its

   ________________ when it's time to hunt.

3. Some animals use color so other animals can't see them. A/An ________________

   that is green can ________________ on a leaf.

3 Match and make logical sentences.

1. Some insects have characteristics
2. A frog has two spots on its back
3. The tiger has stripes on its body
4. Predators try not to be seen when they hunt prey

a. that imitate eyes.
b. that can run or hide when frightened.
c. that help to camouflage it in a jungle.
d. that resemble other poisonous insects.

4 Listen for the puzzle words. Write the matching words under the photos. TR: 06

insect

____

hoverfly resembles

____

tiger predator

____

butterfly spots

____

rabbit prey

____

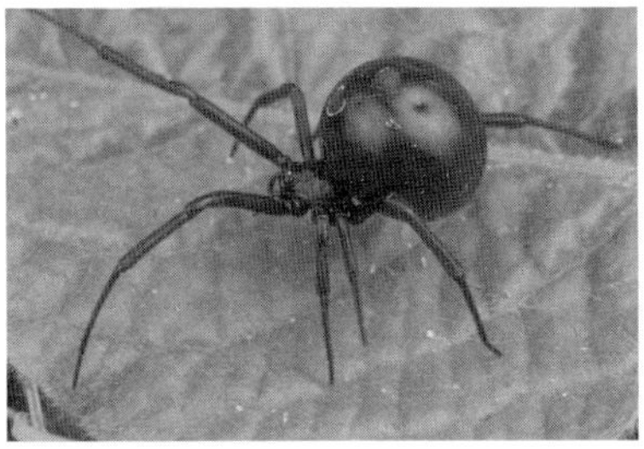

black widow spider species

____

5 Make sentences. Use at least two of these words in each sentence.

camouflage characteristics copy frighten hunt imitate poisonous resemble

1. ______________
2. ______________
3. ______________

6 **Listen and write.** Choose sentences from the song for each picture. **TR: 07**

1. Predators are everywhere, and looking for a feast!
2. ______________________________
3. ______________________________
4. ______________________________

7 **Listen to track 8 again and answer.** Choose words from the song!

1. What do a frog's stripes tell its enemies?

____

2. Why do animals do amazing things?

____

3. What must the predator and prey do each and every day?

____

4. What do animals do to hide in front of our eyes?

____

GRAMMAR

A fox can run **as fast as** a rabbit.

The stripes of some frogs are **as colorful as** a flower.

A three-striped frog is **as poisonous as** a snake.

The spots of a leopard are **as black as** the night.

8 Complete the sentences.

cute dangerous ~~fast~~ green soft

1. A predator must be as fast as its prey.
2. Some insects can be ________ a leaf.
3. The bite of a spider can be ________ the bite of a snake.
4. The fur of a fox is ________ a cat's fur.
5. I think a deer is ________ a dog.

9 Write comparisons.

1. the walk of a duck / funny / a turtle's walk

   The walk of a duck is as funny as a turtle's walk.

2. the wool of an alpaca / soft / a sheep's wool

   ____

3. jaguar / dangerous / a cougar

   ____

4. predator / can be / camouflaged / its prey

   ____

5. a bee sting / painful / a wasp sting

   ____

10 Complete the sentences.

attack avoid confuse defend escape

1. A bird goes under water to __________ an attacking predator.

2. A zebra moves its head to __________ the kick of another zebra.

3. Lions __________ a buffalo.

4. A penguin turns to __________ its nest from a seal.

5. Fish swim in a circle around a hungry seal to __________ it.

6. A baby deer hides in the grass to __________ predators.

11 **Do the puzzle.** Find the hidden word.

camouflage characteristics copies
frighten hide hunt imitates
insect poisonous predator prey
resembles species spots stripes

1) [_] _ _ _
2) _ [_] _ _ _ _
3) [_] _ _ _ _ _
4) [_] _ _ _ _
5) _ _ _ [_] _ _ _ _ _ _
6) _ _ _ _ _ _ _ [_]
7) _ _ _ _ _ _ [_] _
8) _ [_] _ _
9) [_] _ _ _ _ _ _

Hidden word: ______________

1. To a hungry lion, an antelope is ______.
2. One butterfly species ______ the color of another species that tastes bad.
3. This animal is often green or brown and is prey for birds.
4. ______ are round shapes on skin or fur that help camouflage an animal.
5. An animal uses ______ to make it hard to see.
6. A lion walks quietly so that it doesn't ______ its prey.
7. This is an animal that attacks and eats other animals.
8. A hawk flies in a circle to ______ for mice.
9. ______ are long marks on animals.

12 **Work with a partner.** Student 1, go to page 122. Student 2, go to page 124.

GRAMMAR

The spot on that fish **looks** like an eye, **doesn't it?**

The spot on that fish **doesn't** look much like an eye, **does it?**

That deer **will** run into the forest, **won't it?**

That deer **won't** run into the forest, **will it?**

These butterflies **are** beautiful, **aren't they?**

These butterflies **aren't** very beautiful, **are they?**

The coyotes **were** running fast, **weren't they?**

The coyotes **weren't** running very fast, **were they?**

The sting of a bee **can** hurt, **can't it?**

The sting of a bee **can't** hurt much, **can it?**

13 Read and write.

1. The colors are so beautiful, ________________?
2. The spots on the wings look like eyes, ________________?
3. That butterfly doesn't taste bad to predators, ________________?
4. Well, I'm not going to find out myself, ________________?
5. That's a better way of finding the answer to my question, ________________?

14 **Listen and say.** Write the question. TR: 08

1. ______is it______?
2. ________________?
3. ________________?
4. ________________?
5. ________________?
6. ________________?
7. ________________?
8. ________________?

15 **Listen.** Check your answers to Activity 14. TR: 09

16 Complete the sentences.

clear sharp ~~slippery~~ sweet tall

1. A frog is as slippery as a snake, isn't it?
2. The water of some lakes is ________________ glass, ________________?
3. He likes fruit that is ________________ candy, ________________?
4. Your sister is ________________ my sister, ________________?
5. The teeth of a shark can be ________________ a knife, ________________?

17 Read and write.

1. some actors are / famous / the movies they make

   Some actors are as famous as the movies they make, aren't they?
2. his idea is / good / hers

   ____
3. an earache is / bad / a headache

   ____
4. comic books are / fun to read / any book

   ____
5. that blizzard was / cold / an ice storm

   ____

18 Listen and read. TR: 10

Why Do Mockingbirds Copy?

Mockingbirds live in North and South America. They are good copycats. They imitate other birds. But they can also imitate other animals. They can even make sounds that resemble a piano or car alarm. Mockingbirds learn to sing many songs. Some learn more than 200 different songs. They can often trick people! But they can't trick other birds. If mockingbirds can't trick other birds, why do they copy sounds? They do it to attract and avoid other birds!

Males are loud singers and they sing many songs. They always sing when they want to meet females. A male bird can sing most of the day and night. The singing attracts females. But it also keeps away other males. The longer a mockingbird lives, the more songs it knows. To show this characteristic, the male mockingbird sings all the songs it knows. A female mockingbird is attracted to a male who has lived a long time.

Mockingbirds usually sing short songs. They sing each sound several times. Then they move to the next sound. Female mockingbirds sing softly and less often than males. They usually sing at their nests in the winter to keep away other birds. When another bird comes near, the mockingbird makes a loud noise to frighten it.

It's amazing that the mockingbird can copy so many songs of other birds. Some songs are not easy to learn. The mockingbird must listen well to imitate the sounds. But a mockingbird also has good eyes and a good memory. When a person comes near its nest, the mockingbird remembers that person. It knows that person's face after many years!

19 Check T for *True* and F for *False*.

1. The female mockingbird sings more often than the male. Ⓣ Ⓕ
2. When a mockingbird imitates, it often tricks other birds. Ⓣ Ⓕ
3. The female mockingbird sings to attract the male. Ⓣ Ⓕ
4. Mockingbirds can remember human beings. Ⓣ Ⓕ

20 Check what you learned from the text.

Mockingbird characteristic	Male	Female
1. Live in South America		
2. Imitate other birds		
3. Are loud singers		
4. Always sing many songs		
5. Sing to attract		
6. Sing to keep away other birds		

21 List the facts that you know about the lives of mockingbirds.

Use the text in Activity 18 and the chart in Activity 20.

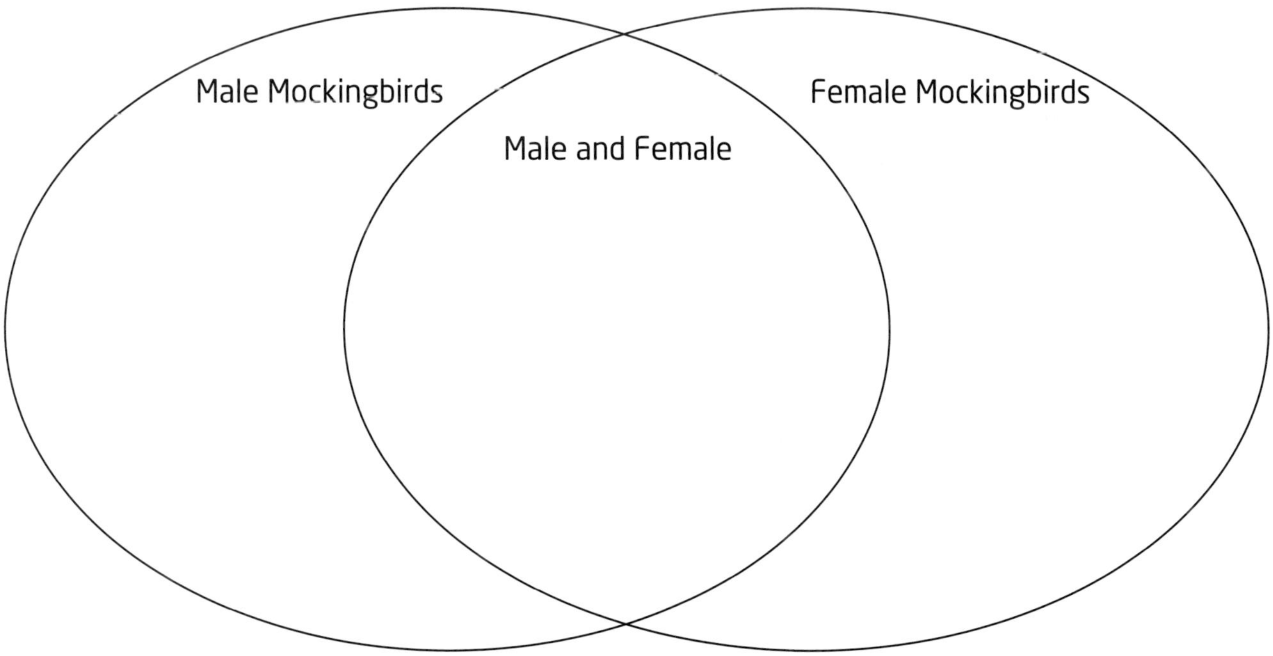

22 Answer the questions in your notebook.

1. What is the most interesting fact you learned about mockingbirds?
2. What other animals can imitate sounds?

23 **Read *One or Two Ways to Imitate* on page 32 of your student book.** How did the writer plan? Read the steps.

1. The writer chose a type of animal. The writer chose *copycat animals.*
2. Next, the writer described the characteristics. *Some animals copy the appearance of other animals. Some animals copy a characteristic like tasting bad or dangerous weapons.*
3. Then the writer wrote about specific animals and described how they copy.

How they look	The viceroy and soldier butterflies resemble each other. The ash borer moth looks like a wasp.
How they taste	The viceroy and soldier butterflies taste bad to predators.
Do they have weapons	The ash borer moth doesn't have a stinger like a wasp.

4. Then the writer wrote a first sentence that says what the paragraph is about. *Some animals copy other animals to avoid attack.*
5. Next, the writer wrote about the characteristics of these types of animals.
6. Finally, the writer wrote sentences about specific animals. To show how these animals belong to a group, the writer used words such as *both, each of, like, but,* and *unlike.*

Imitate in appearance

ash borer moth

wasp

Imitate in appearance and other characteristics

viceroy butterfly

soldier butterfly

24 **Plan to write about animals that have some of the same characteristics.** Take notes.

1. Choose a type of animal ______________________________

2. Describe the characteristics all the animals share. Is it how they look? Is it how they sound? Is it what they can do?

____

25 **Complete the chart.** Write the kind of characteristics you chose in the first column. Write the way the animals share each characteristic in the second column.

How they look	The animals resemble each other.

26 **Now follow steps 1-6 on page 24 to write your paragraph in your notebook.**

27 **Express yourself.** Choose one of the topics below, and write a paragraph of classification. Plan your writing, and follow the steps on page 24. Write your new paragraph in your notebook.

- cats and dogs
- apples and oranges
- pens and pencils

Unit 3

Music in Our World

1 **Look and listen.** Write the words that you hear. **TR: 11**

band	beat	chord	concert	drum	~~flute~~	guitar	lead singer
melody	note	perform	piano	~~practice~~	rhythm	saxophone	violin

1 

practice

flute

2 

____

____

3 

____

____

4 

____

____

5 

____

____

6 

____

____

7 

____

____

8 

____

____

2 Unscramble and write.

Mei is the *dlae nregsi* ________________ in a *danb* ________________. There are four other musicians who play with her. Feng plays the *murd* ________________. He makes the *tbae* ________________ for the group. Xui Li plays *srodch* ________________ with the *rtaugi* ________________ to make the *mythhr* ________________. Ting plays each *ento* ________________ of the *yoldme* ________________ with her *hoopnxase* ________________. And Xu Guan plays both the *opnai* ________________ and the *oliivn* ________________. The music sounds great because they *tarpccie* ________________ a lot! They *rorpfem* ________________ at a *ecctnor* ________________ today.

3 Read the words in the box. Write the words in the correct column.

beat chord drum flute guitar melody note piano saxophone violin

Instruments	Parts of Music

4 Underline the best answer.

1. play an instrument for others to hear (perform / practice)
2. play an instrument to get better at it (perform / practice)
3. a thing used to make music (lead singer / instrument)
4. a person who uses the voice to make music (lead singer / instrument)

5 **Listen to the song.** Answer the song questions in order. **TR: 12**

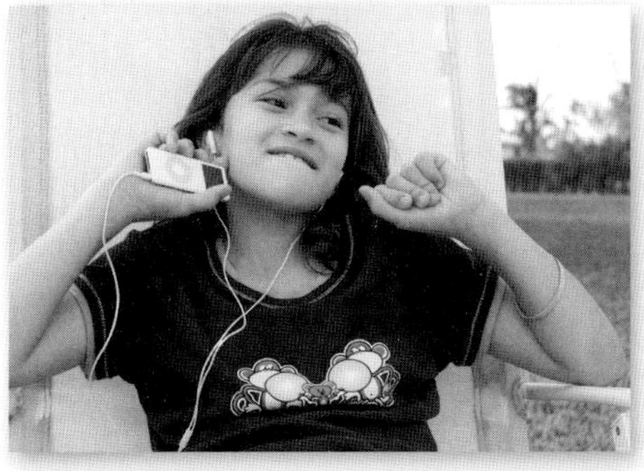

1. Have you ever listened to ___hip-hop___ ?

   Yes, I have. / No, I haven't.

2. Have you ever listened to ____________?

   ____

3. I can hear the ____________. Can you?

   ____

4. Have you ever played a ____________?

   ____

5. Have you ever played a ____________?

   ____

6. Have you ever played a ____________?

   ____

6 **Read and write.** Write new verses for the song.

Listen to the rhythm.	Listen to the ____________.
Listen to that band!	Listen to that ____________!
Sing the notes	Sing the ____________
and clap your hands.	and ____________.
The flute is playing.	The ____________ is playing.
The piano is, too.	The ____________ is, too.
I can hear the guitar.	I can hear the ____________.
Can you?	Can you?

GRAMMAR

Has	she	**ever**	**played**	the piano?
Have	you	**ever**	**sung**	a pop song?
I	**have**	**never**	**sung**	a hip-hop song.
She	**has**	**never**	**played**	the guitar.

7 Read and write

1. Have we ever been there?
   No, we have never been there ______.
2. ______
   No, she has never listened to a flute.
3. ______
   No, he has never played a chord on the guitar.
4. ______
   No, I have never been to a concert.
5. Have they ever practiced together?
   No, ______.

GRAMMAR

This is the first time she **has ever** played the piano.

8 **Read and write.** Write your own sentences.

1. This is the first time my teacher ______.
2. It's the only time I ______.
3. That's the first time my friends ______.
4. This is the only time my brother ______.

9 **Work with a partner.** Ask and answer. Take turns.

Have you ever written a song before?

No, I have never written a song before!

10 **Look and match.** Write the name of the type of music. Then write the names of performers you know in each column.

classical hip-hop jazz pop rock

1. 

____

2. 

____

3. 

____

4. 

____

5. 

____

hip-hop	classical	rock	jazz	pop

11 **Listen.** Number the music styles in the order you hear them. **TR: 13**

☐ classical ☐ hip-hop ☐ jazz ☐ pop ☐ rock

12 Read and write. Read the second paragraph on page 38 of your Student Book. Write the words on the fish. Put them in order.

beat chord melody note rhythm

13 Complete the sentences.

saxophone concert band rhythm lead singer practice

1. You can be a ________________.
2. You can start a ________________ with others.
3. You can ________________ to get better.
4. You can go to a ________________.

14 Choose and write. Choose two words from the box. Write a sentence with the two words.

band	beat	classical	concert	drum	flute	guitar
hip-hop	jazz	lead singer	perform	pop	rock	saxophone

1. I want to play the guitar in a rock band!
2. ____
3. ____
4. ____
5. ____

GRAMMAR

You broke a string! You should play **more carefully**! (+)

Can you play that song **more slowly**? (+)

I play jazz **better than** my brother does. (+)

He plays the guitar **less often than** he plays the piano. (–)

Ines can sing **as well as** Marison can. (=)

Mario doesn't sing **as beautifully as** his brother. (=)

well → **better**

badly → **worse**

fast → **faster/ less fast**

slowly → **more/less slowly**

frequently → **more/ less frequently**

15 Complete the sentences.

1. He can perform ________________ the other musicians if he practices. (=, well)
2. She plays classical music ________________ pop music. (-, often)
3. He plays the violin ________________ he plays other string instruments. (+, well)
4. He moves his right hand ________________ his left hand. (+, fast)
5. I play the guitar ________________ I play the bass. (-, frequently)

16 **Read and write.** Write sentences using comparisons.

1. Hsin plays the piano well. Hua plays the piano better.
   Hua plays the piano better than Hsin.
2. He practices the first song often. He practices the last song less often.
   ____
   ____
3. We can sing well. They can sing well.
   ____
4. I like to listen to rock music. I like to listen to hip-hop music a little less.
   ____
   ____
5. Pang goes to concerts two times per year. Ming goes to concerts three times per year.
   ____
   ____

17 **Read and write.** Complete the conversation with words from the box.

better than ever more often than never

Marta: Have you ________ been sad and listened to music to make you happy?

Carla: Yes! Few things work ________ music to change how you feel. There's a song my grandma taught me. If I'm sad, I want to hear it ________ any other song! Has this ________ happened to you?

Marta: Yes! Have you ________ heard a song called *Somewhere Over the Rainbow*?

Carla: No, I've ________ heard it.

Marta: You should listen to it!

18 **Listen and write.** TR: 14

1. Has Raul ever played that beat faster than Maria? No, he hasn't.
2. Have you ever heard me play louder? ________
3. Has he ever practiced as much as this week? ________
4. Does Roberto ever play music softer? ________
5. Does Carmen ever sing worse than Alexa? ________

19 **Find someone in the class that has never done these things.**

ride a bike ________ play basketball ________

have cereal for breakfast ________ listen to hip-hop ________

go to a classical concert ________ sleep until eleven ________

Markus, have you ever ridden a bike?

Yes, I have!

Alex, have you ever ridden a bike?

No, I haven't.

20 **Listen and read.** TR: 15

Listen to This!

"Hey, turn that music down!"

Do you ever wonder why your parents tell you to turn the volume down when you're listening to loud music on your MP3? It's not because they don't like the rhythm and melody. (Well, hip-hop *might* not be their favorite music!) It's important to listen to music and other sounds at the right volume because if you don't, it can hurt your ears!

Did you know that sound travels in waves? These waves can move fast or slow, depending on their frequency. The type of sound that these waves make when they move is called pitch. If a sound wave moves slowly, the pitch is low, like the sound of someone playing a bass guitar. If a sound wave moves quickly, the pitch is high, like the sound of someone playing a flute or violin.

Sometimes, a sound has a frequency that is too high or too low for people to hear. We measure frequency in hertz. The range that humans can hear is 20–20,000 hertz (Hz). Dolphins can hear sounds from 75–200,000 Hz! That means they can hear things we can't.

We measure the volume of a sound in decibels (dB). The sound of people whispering is about 30 dB, the sound of a rock concert is closer to 115 dB, and the sound of a jet engine is about 140 dB! The max output of most MP3 players is between 70–90 dB, which is really loud! Try to keep the volume at 50 dB instead. Your ears will thank you!

Elephant
5-10,000 Hz

Dog
40-60,000 Hz

Dolphin
75-200,000 Hz

21 Check T for *True* and F for *False*.

1. Sound travels in waves. (T) (F)
2. If a sound wave moves slowly, the pitch is high. (T) (F)
3. A violin has a higher pitch than a bass guitar. (T) (F)
4. People can hear sounds that are too high for dolphins. (T) (F)

22 Correct the false sentences in Activity 21.

____

____

23 Match the words to the definitions.

1. pitch	a. unit used to measure frequency
2. frequency	b. the position of a sound in a range from low to high
3. decibel	c. the speed at which sound waves move
4. hertz	d. unit used to measure the volume of a sound

24 Label the graph.

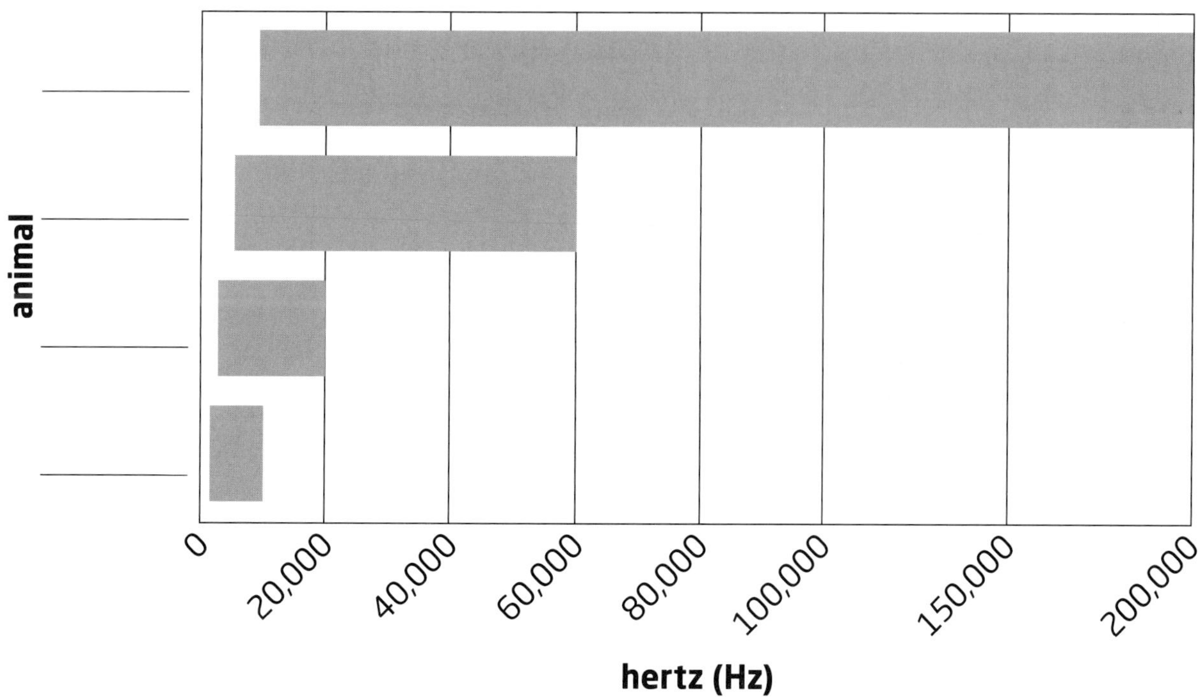

25 Read *Composing, Then and Now* on page 48 of your Student Book.

How did the writer plan? Read the steps.

1. The writer chose the topic of composing.
2. Next, the writer chose a contrast in that topic: composing in the past and composing now.
3. Then the writer wrote different facts about the past and now.

Composing Then	Composing Now
1. Composers used pen and paper.	1. Composers use computer and phone apps.
2. Composers wrote notes on lined measures of music.	2. Composers hum a song and the app writes the notes.

4. The writer chose words of contrast to show differences: *but now, although, more and more, before, in contrast, in the past, while.*
5. Next, the writer started the paragraph with two contrasting sentences to show what the paragraph is about. *In the past, composers traditionally created their music with paper and pen. But now,...*
6. Then the writer contrasted other characteristics of composing in the past and composing now.
7. Finally, the writer wrote a sentence to close the paragraph. *While a traditional composer is busy cleaning ink off fingers, a modern composer can write more songs instead!*

26 Plan to write about two styles of music or two instruments.

1. Circle your topic. two styles of music two instruments
2. Write the main facts you want to contrast.

First music style or instrument ________________	Second music style or instrument ________________
1.	1.
2.	2.

27 **Choose words of contrast to show differences.** Use them to contrast the information in the chart.

1. ____

____

2. ____

____

28 **Write more characteristics of the things you are contrasting.**

First style or musical instrument

1. ____
2. ____
3. ____

Second style or musical instrument

1. ____
2. ____
3. ____

29 **Now follow steps 2-7 on page 36.** Write your paragraph of contrast in your notebook.

30 **Express yourself.** Choose a topic below to write about *then* and *now*. Plan your writing and follow the steps on page 36. Write your new paragraph in your notebook.

Cooking meals, then and now

Having fun, then and now

Going somewhere, then and now

Using a telephone, then and now

Unit 4

Life Out There

1 **Do a puzzle.** Read the clues. Fill in the words.

atmosphere
comet
data
debate
extraterrestrials
galaxy
journey
orbit
planet
solar system
space
universe

Across

1. People ______ whether there is life beyond Earth.
6. Mars travels in a(n) ______ around the sun.
7. information = ______
10. Earth is the third ______ from the sun.
11. The ______ is made of space and all the stars.
12. Earth's ______ is like a blanket that protects us.

Down

2. If ______ exist, they live in other places beyond Earth.
3. A(n) ______ is a trip from one place to another.
4. The ______ is made up of a sun and the planets that go around it.
5. We sent rockets into ______.
8. A big group of stars is known as a(n) ______.
9. A(n) ______ is a moving cloud of rock, ice, and gas.

2 Complete the sentences.

atmosphere	data	debate
extraterrestrials	orbit	solar system

1. Venus is a planet in our ______________.
2. Venus travels around the sun in a closer ______________ than Earth.
3. Venus has a(n) ______________ that hides the planet's surface.
4. Scientists have sent instruments to Venus to collect ______________.
5. Do you think ______________ can live on Venus?
6. You believe it and I don't. We can ______________ the topic to decide who is right.

3 **Work with a partner.** Ask and answer.

How can you describe . . .

1. an extraterrestrial?
2. space?
3. an orbit?
4. the atmosphere?
5. a comet?
6. the universe?

4 **Listen to the song.** Match to complete. **TR: 18**

1. But right here on planet Earth
2. Let's all take a journey
3. We might find things we've never seen
4. We might find a moon
5. beyond our solar system,

a. deep in outer space.
b. where flowers grow.
c. life is all around.
d. far away from here
e. past the atmosphere.

5 **Read and match.** Write a sentence from Activity 4 that matches each picture.

1. ______________________________
2. ______________________________
3. ______________________________

6 **Listen and write.** Listen to track 18 again. List some things the song says we might find. Then write a new verse!

1. We might find ______ a moon ______.
2. We might find ______________________.
3. We might find ______________________.
4. We might find ______________________.

____

____

____

GRAMMAR

We **may** travel to another solar system.	We **might** travel to another solar system.
A planet **may** orbit that star. Some data point to it.	A planet **might** orbit that star. There's not much data, though.
I think it **may** be a comet.	I thought it **might** be a comet.
She knows that planets **may** orbit that star.	She knew that planets **might** orbit that star.

7 Write sentences that say you're not sure.

1. We have a debate tomorrow. We may/might have a debate tomorrow.
2. That star has planets. ______
3. The universe is bigger than you think. ______
4. The comet's orbit goes outside the solar system. ______
5. That planet has an atmosphere. ______

8 Read and write. Use the word(s) in parentheses to finish each sentence.

1. We heard that extraterrestrials (*live*) might live on other planets.
2. I see that a planet (*be next to*) ______.
3. He knows that a comet (*fly across*) ______.
4. She thought that the debate (*end*) ______.
5. I think that the data (*not be*) ______.

9 Work with a partner. Ask about what you'll do tonight. Answer to say you're not sure. Take turns.

Will you look for comets in the sky tonight?

I might look for comets in the sky tonight.

10 **Read and look.** Match each picture with a sentence.

1. The rocket fires and lifts the spacecraft away from Earth.
2. The astronaut searches her instruments.
3. An astronaut at the space station communicates with scientists.

11 **Read and write.**

astronaut communicate search spacecraft space station

1. You ______________ to find something.
2. You ______________ when you want to tell someone something.
3. A(n) ______________ is a person who travels in space.
4. The ______________ orbits Earth, and people live and work in it.
5. A(n) ______________ carries people into space and back.

12 **Solve the riddles.** Choose the word pair that matches the description in each riddle.

astronaut/rocket search/communicate spacecraft/space station

1. You can do one of these things alone. The other thing needs two or more people. ______________
2. You can be one of these things. You can travel inside the other thing.

   ____
3. You can travel inside one of these things. You can live in the other thing.

   ____

13 **Read.** Underline the correct words.

1. Two planets in our *universe / solar system* orbit the sun closer than Earth.
2. A *comet / planet* may need an atmosphere to support life.
3. We use radios to *communicate / journey* with spacecraft.
4. Scientists collect *search / data* to look for life on other planets.
5 Astronauts use a spacecraft to get to the *rocket / space station.*
6. We have sent *astronauts / extraterrestrials* into space.
7. Scientists use SETI to *search / debate* for extraterrestrial intelligence.
8. Some *spacecraft / comets* have big orbits that go outside of the solar system.

14 **Read.** Draw lines to match.

1. Let's take a journey	a. with atmospheres.
2. Let's use a rocket	b. to send up our spacecraft.
3. Let's travel past	c. communicate back to Earth.
4. Let's find new data to	d. about extraterrestrials!
5. Let's search for planets	e. into space.
6. Let's end the debate	f. the moon and the planets.

15 **Read and write.** Use each word twice to complete the sentences.

debate orbit search

1. Two moons ____________ the planet Mars.
2. Scientists look for data in their ____________ for intelligent life.
3. The Mars rover, called *Curiosity*, may ____________ Mars for water.
4. Scientists do not agree. They ____________ whether life was ever on Mars.
5. You can see Mars in its ____________ around the sun.
6. You can go to the ____________ and say that Mars never had life on it.

GRAMMAR

Jiao, Lan, Gao, and Zhuang want to fly in a spaceship.	**Everyone** wants to fly in a spaceship.
Jiao or Lan or Gao or Zhuang can be an astronaut.	**Anyone** can be an astronaut.
Zhuang is tall.	**Someone** is tall.
Jiao, Lan, Gao, and Zhuang are not adults.	**No one** is an adult.

16 **Look and write.** Tell about the picture.

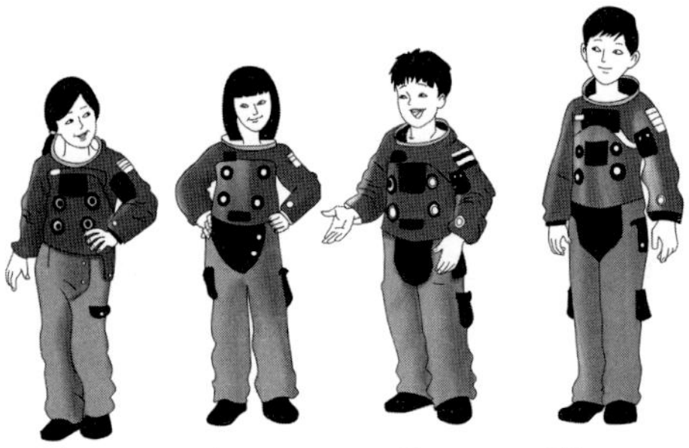

anyone everyone no one someone

1. __________ is sitting down.
2. Maybe __________ told a joke because Gao is laughing.
3. I don't see __________ wearing a helmet.
4. __________ is dressed as an astronaut.

17 **Read and write.** Use the words from Activity 16 to complete each sentence.

1. I will be the only one home. __________ else will be at work or school.
2. Be careful and don't lose your book. Don't give it to __________.
3. It is very late. __________ is on the phone at this hour.
4. I don't know if it's Hugo or Luis, but I hear __________ calling my name.

18 **Listen and circle the answer.** TR: 19

1. *Everyone* / *Someone* wants to go to the planetarium.
2. *Someone* / *No one* saw the comet.
3. *Anyone* / *Someone* can answer that question.
4. I want to invite *someone* / *everyone* to come with me.

19 **Look and listen.** Number the words in the order you first hear them. **TR: 20**

☐ anyone

☐ everyone

☐ no one

☐ someone

☐ may

20 **Listen again.** Answer each question with a sentence. **TR: 21**

1. Who might come as an extraterrestrial?

____

2. Who can people at the party dress like?

____

3. What is the boy worried about?

____

4. Who may come, too?

____

21 **Work with a partner.** Student 1, go to page 123 and ask a question. Student 2, go to page 125 and say the matching sentence. Take turns.

Can everyone see the comet in the sky?

We may all be able to see it if the sky is not cloudy.

22 Listen and read. TR: 22

Life on Mars

Mars is the fourth planet from the sun, just after Earth. You can see Mars without a telescope, but you need a telescope to see its characteristics. Many years ago, people began looking at Mars with a telescope. They wondered if Mars ever had life.

In 1877, an Italian scientist, Giovanni Schiaparelli, saw what he thought were canals on the surface of Mars. Canals are like rivers but made by people. They let boats make the journey from one place to another. People thought that Martians may have dug the canals!

When telescopes got better, people forgot the canal idea. In 1965, the spacecraft *Mariner 4* flew by Mars and took photos. The photos showed that the surface looks a lot like Earth's moon. It has lots of marks from rocks hitting it. Today, no one thinks that Mars has extraterrestrials.

In 2012, the Mars rover *Curiosity* landed on Mars. It sent a lot of data back to Earth. Some data may show that tiny life once lived on Mars long ago. Scientists still debate this. Scientists will be studying Mars for many years to come.

23 Check T for *True* and F for *False*.

1. Mars has canals that are like rivers. Ⓣ Ⓕ
2. In 1877, *Mariner 4* flew by Mars and took photos. Ⓣ Ⓕ
3. Some data may show that life on Mars might be possible. Ⓣ Ⓕ
4. Scientists don't know if there was ever life on Mars. Ⓣ Ⓕ

24 Read and write.

1. You can see Mars without a __________.
2. People thought that they saw __________ on Mars, but they were wrong.
3. The surface of Mars has marks from falling rocks like Earth's __________.
4. It's possible that there was __________ on Mars many years ago.

25 **Complete the chart.** Use information from Activity 22.

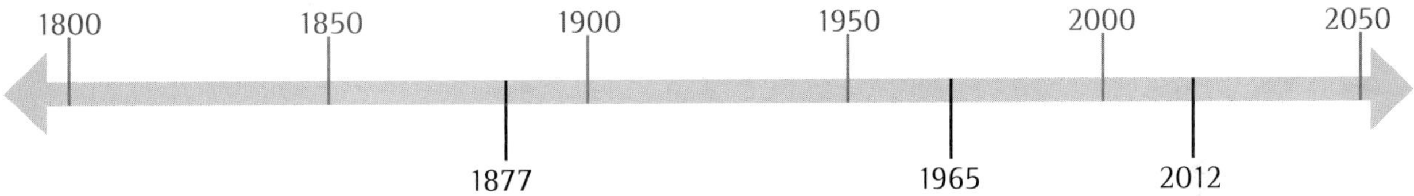

__________	__________	__________
__________	__________	__________
__________	__________	__________

26 **Read and answer.** Use information from Activity 22.

1. What are canals? __________
2. Mars does not have canals. What helped people learn this?

   ____
3. Why does the land on Mars look like Earth's moon?

   ____
4. What could data from the Mars rover *Curiosity* tell us?

   ____

27 **Work with a partner.** Discuss the following.

- Something you already knew about Mars.
- Something you just learned about Mars.
- Something you'd like to learn about Mars.

28 Read *Forever Searching* on page 68 of your Student Book.

How did the writer plan? Read the steps below.

1. First, the writer chose an opinion. What was the writer's opinion?

   People are forever searching. We search both on Earth and in space because ______________________________

   ____

   ____

2. Second, the writer wrote down facts that support the opinion.

Opinion	Supporting Facts
We have always been people who search.	______________ searched the stars. Zheng traveled to ______________. Cook went to the ______________. Amundsen traveled to the ______________.

3. Third, the writer wrote expressions to introduce the facts. Look for the following expressions in the story.

   Long ago, research shows, the facts show

4. Fourth, the writer wrote a strong conclusion.

   We search both on Earth and in space because we like to find answers. And a big question is, are we alone? We will search until we know.

5. Finally, the writer organized the sentences in a draft, or a first version, of the passage. The writer started with an example.

   Example: *Long ago, people thought that the sun and planets orbited Earth.*

   An example is a good way to introduce a topic. You can decide to start with an example or with an introduction to the main idea.

   Introduction to main idea: *Why do we search? The facts show that we have always been people who search.*

29 **Should we search for life in space?** Look at Activity 20 in your Student Book. Write what you think. Should we search for life in space or not?

____

____

30 **Follow steps 2-5 on page 52.** Use the space below to plan. Then write your paragraphs in your notebook.

Opinions	Supporting Facts

Write expressions that introduce:

____

Write a strong conclusion:

____

31 **Express yourself.** Choose one of the topics below, and write a paragraph that persuades. Plan your writing, and follow the steps on page 52. Write your new paragraph in your notebook.

There may (or may not) be life on other planets.
It may be good (or bad) for people to find life on other planets.
Space exploration helps (or doesn't help) people on Earth.
Learning about other planets is (or is not) important for people on Earth.

Unit 5

Arts Lost and Found

1 **Read and write.** Choose the word that best describes each list of words.

art community ~~culture~~ language traditions

1. education, laws, music, clothing, beliefs ___culture___
2. Spanish, Arabic, Chinese, Japanese ________________
3. painting, drawing, coloring ________________
4. stores, hospitals, schools, sports teams ________________
5. cooking for holidays, singing songs, telling stories ________________

2 **Read and complete the sentences.**

hold on passed down proud share

1. I feel good about my family. I am ________________ of my family.
2. My father is a farmer. I want to be a farmer, too. When I'm older, I hope the farm is ________________ to me by my father.
3. I cut my apple in half to give some to my sister. I ________________ my apple with my sister.
4. My family sings together every Sunday. I want to ________________ to that tradition and continue to sing every Sunday.

3 **Label the pictures.** Match the words to each picture.

hold on   pass down   share   storytelling   tourists   weave

____

____

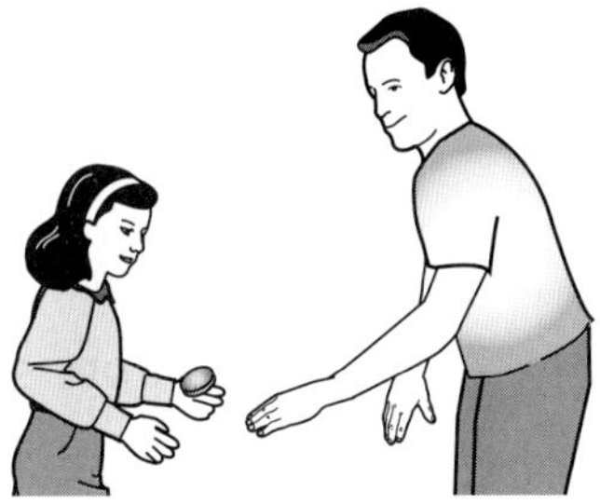

____

____

____

____

4 **Listen and write.** Write the words in the order you hear them. **TR: 23**

art   community   culture   future   generation
language   local   proud   traditions

1. ______________
2. ______________
3. ______________
4. ______________
5. ______________
6. ______________
7. ______________
8. ______________
9. ______________

5 **What can you say?** Use the words to write sentences.

1. future / art I think about the future of art in our country.
2. pass down / traditions ______________
3. storytelling / share ______________
4. tourists / weave ______________
5. hold on / culture ______________

6 **Listen to the song.** Use the words in the box to complete the verses. **TR: 24**

art	culture	family	holding on
pride	storytelling	weaving	

Knowing your history is important.

__________ to your culture is an excellent thing!

Knowing your history is important.

It's up to you to keep your __________ strong!

What special __________ does your culture bring to our world?

What special thing does your __________ bring to our world?

__________? Learn to do it!

__________? Learn to tell it!

What brings your culture __________?

7 **Listen again.** Check **T** for *True* and **F** for *False*. **TR: 25**

1. It isn't very important to know your history. (T) (F)
2. You don't need to keep your culture strong. (T) (F)
3. Culture can bring art to the world. (T) (F)
4. You learn to sew to do embroidery. (T) (F)

8 **Remember and write.** List four things from the song you can learn. Then write two new lines for the song.

1. Learn to sculpt it! sculpture
2. Learn to tell it! __________
3. Learn to sew it! __________
4. Learn to do it! __________

____

____

GRAMMAR

Sharing traditions is fun.

Weaving takes a long time to learn.

Running is good exercise.

Making a paper airplane takes practice.

9 **Read.** Complete the sentences.

communicate debate ~~hold on~~ pass down search

1. ___Holding on___ to traditions is very important!
2. ________ my grandfather's clock to me made my father happy.
3. ________ by telephone is harder in another language.
4. ________ for a good song to sing is exciting.
5. ________ is one way to learn how someone else thinks.

10 **What about you?** Complete each sentence about you and your friends or family.

1. Walking ________.
2. Writing ________.
3. Watching TV ________.
4. Cleaning ________.
5. Eating ________.
6. Drawing ________.

11 **Complete the story.**

making painting storytelling weaving writing

________ things is a proud tradition in my family. We all have our own jobs to do. ________ is my grandmother's job. She made this shirt for me. Grandpa likes to talk and knows lots of stories. ________ is always his job. I'm good with a paintbrush, so ________ is what I do. My sister doesn't talk much, but she also likes to make up stories. ________ is her hobby.

12 **Read and look.** Match each word with a picture.

embroidery
handcrafted
jewelry making
pottery
sculpture

1

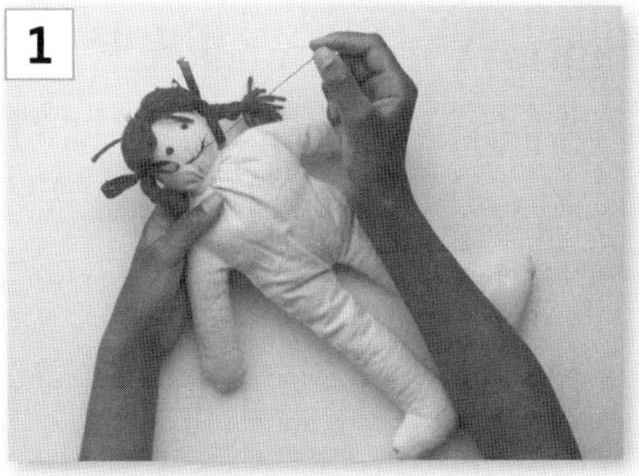

____

2

____

3

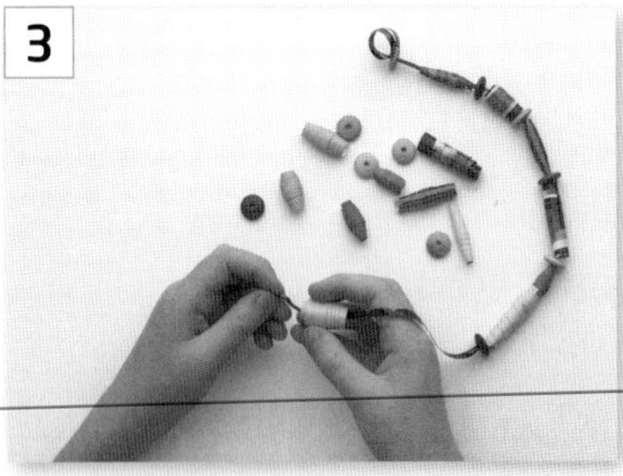

____

4

____

5

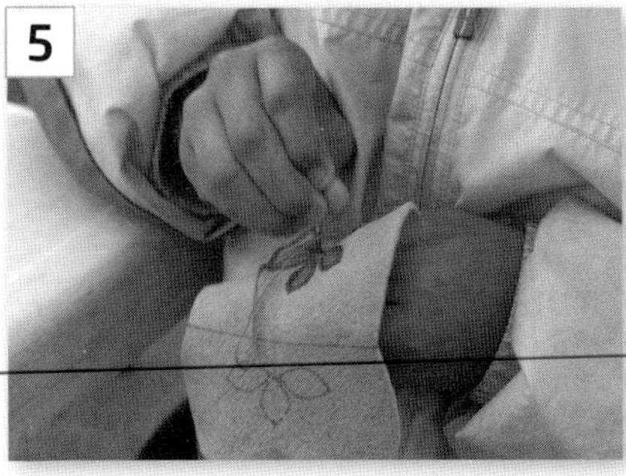

____

13 **Read and complete.** Use words from Activity 12.

Salma: That ring is so pretty! Is it made of gold?

Aisha: Yes, my uncle made it. He often uses gold for ______________.

Salma: Your uncle made it by hand?

Aisha: Yes, this ring is ______________ by my uncle.

Salma: My uncle is an artist, too! He works with clay.

Aisha: What does he make? Does he make dishes and cups?

Salma: Yes, he makes ______________ with clay. He also makes animals and people with clay.

Aisha: Oh wow! He makes clay ______________! Does he make dolls, too?

Salma: Yes, and my aunt makes clothes for the dolls. Some have colorful ______________ on them.

Aisha: I'd love to see one of those dolls!

14 **Read.** Underline the correct words.

1. A basket can be made by *embroidering / weaving* thin strips of plants.
2. A mother can *hold on / pass down* her jewelry to her children.
3. People who live here speak the *tourist / local* language.
4. A doctor is important to the *community / storytelling.*
5. My uncle is part of my father's *generation / language.*
6. I am *holding on / proud* of my cultural traditions.
7. We can hold on to the past as we build our *share / future.*
8. This is the *pottery / jewelry* we use for dinner.

15 **Listen.** Check **T** for *True* and **F** for *False.* **TR: 26**

1. (T) (F)	3. (T) (F)	5. (T) (F)	7. (T) (F)
2. (T) (F)	4. (T) (F)	6. (T) (F)	8. (T) (F)

16 **Work with a partner.** Student 1, go to the bottom of page 123 and ask a question. Student 2, go to the bottom of page 125 and look at the pictures and answer. Take turns.

GRAMMAR

Paolo is tired of **weaving** the long tablecloth.

Susanna thanked her sister for **making** the jewelry.

You like **speaking** English.

I remember **cooking** fish with you on our last trip.

17 **Look and write.** Tell about the pictures.

~~good at/hit~~	likes/play	enjoys/make
loves/swim	interested in/learn	excited about/go

She is good at hitting the ball.

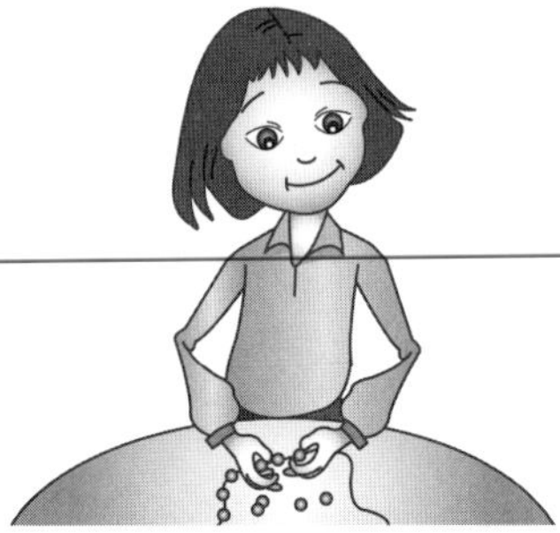

18 **Read and write the correct words.** Then listen and check your answers. **TR: 27**

1. (*Hit* / *Kick*) __________ the TV with your hand won't turn it on!
2. I'm interested in (*read* / *watch*) __________ the ball game.
3. Have you tried (*lift* / *push*) __________ the green button?
4. No. Do you think (*try* / *write*) __________ that button will start the TV?
5. Of course! I always turn it on by (*run* / *use*) __________ the green button.
6. You were right! My TV turns on by (*touch* / *scratch*) __________ the bottom of the screen.
7. Your TV is newer, but I like (*show* / *learn*) __________ people how it works.
8. Thanks for (*help* / *know*) __________ me!

19 **Read and write.** Choose the best word to complete the sentences correctly.

1. ___Telling___ stories is hard to do well. I like ___listening___ to stories! (*listen* / *tell*)
2. __________ soup on cold days can keep you warm. I also think __________ on a sweater can help you keep warm. (*put* / *eat*)
3. I heard you __________ with Paula. She likes __________ jokes. (*laugh* / *tell*)
4. __________ is the best way to stay healthy. I like __________ to the pool. (*go* / *swim*)
5. __________ baseball taught me how to catch a ball. __________ the ball is much harder. (*hit* / *play*)
6. __________ your culture keeps it alive for the next generation. I think that __________ about culture is important. (*learn* / *pass down*)

20 **Read and write.** Write sentences about what you like or enjoy.

1. Playing the guitar is fun! I enjoy playing the guitar with my brother.
2. ______________________________
3. ______________________________
4. ______________________________
5. ______________________________

21 **Listen and read.** TR: 28

Legong Dance

Legong dance is a cultural tradition in Bali, Indonesia. Only young girls perform this dance. Their costumes are beautiful and colorful! The young dancers move slowly to traditional music. The musicians play drums, flutes, and gongs. The dancers tell a story with their faces, hands, and fingers. Every move has a special meaning.

Legong dance teaches people traditional stories. In one story, a king falls in love with a princess! The dancers perform for an hour. However, the dances are too long for many tourists. Shows for them last only 15 minutes, they tell only a part of a story, and they are performed by older dancers. The money from tourists is important because it attracts new dancers to Legong dance.

It is hard to hold on to traditions such as this because many people enjoy listening to newer music. If local people aren't interested in the dances, then they might not be passed down to younger generations. Changing the tradition helps keep Legong dance alive. Today, more people are learning the dances, and there are more performances of Legong dance. More people can watch and learn about this beautiful tradition.

22 **Check T for *True* and F for *False*.**

1. Legong dance is performed in Indonesia. (T) (F)
2. People of all ages can become Legong dancers. (T) (F)
3. Tourists like watching long performances of Legong dance. (T) (F)
4. It is easy to hold on to traditions such as the Legong dance. (T) (F)

23 **Complete the chart.** Use information from Activity 21.

Sights of Legong Dance	Sounds of Legong Dance
The young dancers move slowly.	

24 **Read and answer.**

1. What did you learn about the Legong dance tradition?

____

2. Why do some shows last only 15 minutes?

____

3. Why is story important in Legong dance?

____

4. Why is money important for Legong dancers?

____

25 **Work with a partner.** Complete the chart. Compare the traditional dance to the dance for tourists. Is money from tourists good or bad for Legong dance? Why?

Traditional Legong Dance	Legong Dance for Tourists
The dance is ____________ long.	The dance is ____________ minutes long.
The dancers are ____________.	The dancers are older.
The dance tells ______________.	The dance tells part of a story.
Dancers don't get much money.	Dancers get more money from tourists.

26 **Read *Cecilia's Blog* on page 84 of your Student Book.** How did the writer plan her writing? Read the steps below.

1. First, the writer chose a topic. What was the topic? ______________________________

2. Second, the writer wrote a step-by-step description of what she did.

a. took a long train ride

b. took a bus

c. the bus went up the mountain

d. arrived at Machu Picchu

e. climbed the stairs to the Sun Gate

f. stopped to rest

g. could see everything at the top

3. Third, the writer wrote her thoughts and feelings: *It was awesome!, I was excited., It was so cool., I was incredibly tired., It was wonderful.*

4. Fourth, the writer asked the reader to post a response.

   What did the writer ask the reader? ______________________________

5. Finally, the writer wrote a sentence of introduction and organized the sentences in a draft, or a first version, of the paragraph.

   My family and I went to Machu Picchu in Peru.

27 **Write a blog.** Look at Activity 19 in your Student Book. Choose a topic about a family vacation or special day.

____

28 Follow steps 2–5 on page 64. Use the space below to plan. Write your blog entry in your notebook.

a. ____________________

b. ____________________

c. ____________________

d. ____________________

e. ____________________

f. ____________________

g. ____________________

Write your thoughts and feelings: ____________________

Write a sentence that asks for a response: ____________________

29 **Express yourself.** Choose one of the topics below, and write a blog entry. Plan your writing, and follow the steps on page 64. Write your new blog entry in your notebook.

Write about something you did with a friend or group of friends.

Write about something new you recently learned.

Write about a problem you want to solve.

Unit 1 Student 1, use with Activity 14 on page 7.

14 **Ask and answer the questions together.** Use the words in parentheses and the sentences below the box.

1. How cold is it today? (and)

   The temperature dropped four degrees, and it ended up at fifteen degrees.

2. Did the storm have thunder and lightning? (but)

   ____

3. What did you bring for the storm? (we)

   ____

4. Was there a storm with high winds? (with)

   ____

5. What was the range of temperatures yesterday? (and)

   ____

1. The temperature dropped four degrees.
2. The storm was too far to see lightning.
3. I brought a flashlight.
4. There were very strong winds.
5. The temperature dropped to eighteen degrees.

Unit 2 Student 1, use with Activity 12 on page 19.

12 **Ask and answer.** Ask each other questions about these animal adaptations.

Why do many animals have whiskers?

To find out if they can fit into a specific area.

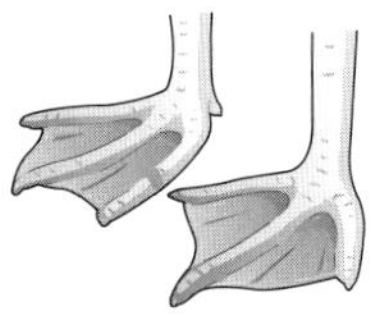

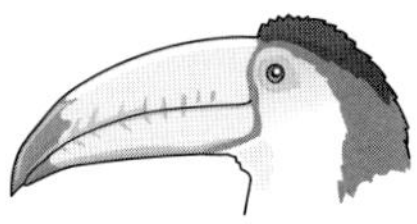

Unit 4 Student 1, use with Activity 21 on page 49.

21 **Ask and answer.** Ask your partner one question. Respond to your partner's question with the correct answer from the list below. Take turns.

Questions:

1. Can everyone see the comet in the sky?
2. Can someone breathe on another planet?
3. Does no one want to take a journey to Mars?
4. Does anyone know how far Earth is from the sun?

Answers for your partner:

a. I may watch it after I finish my school work.
b. Some people say we should only think about Earth.
c. Data from intelligent life may be hidden by noise in space.
d. Maria says she wants to visit another planet.

Unit 5 Student 1, use with Activity 16 on page 59.

16 **Ask and answer.** Ask your partner a question about a picture on the left. Respond to your partner's question with the correct answer from the right. Take turns.

1

Embroider on clothing.

a

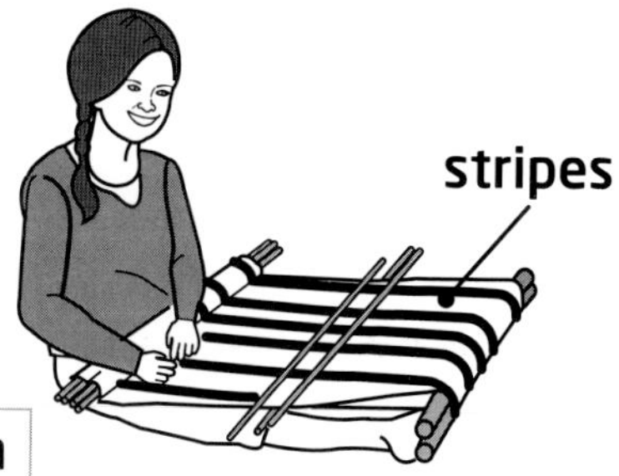

2

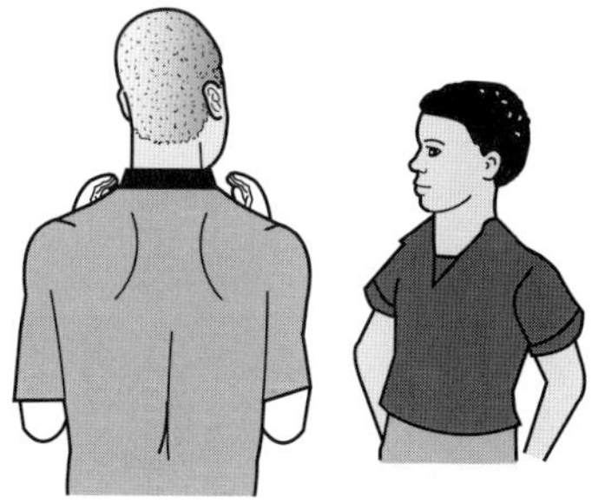

Show pride in local art.

b

Unit 1 Student 2, use with Activity 14 on page 7.

14 **Ask and answer the questions together.** Use the words in parentheses and the sentences below the box.

1. How cold is it today? (and)

   The temperature dropped four degrees, and it ended up at fifteen degrees.
2. Did the storm have thunder and lightning? (but)

   ____
3. What did you bring for the storm? (we)

   ____
4. Was there a storm with high winds? (with)

   ____
5. What was the range of temperatures yesterday? (and)

   ____

1. The temperature ended up at fifteen degrees.
2. There was thunder.
3. I brought supplies, including food and water.
4. There was a hurricane.
5. The temperature rose to twenty-two degrees.

Unit 2 Student 2, use with Activity 12 on page 19.

12 **Ask and answer.** Ask each other questions about these animal adaptations.

Unit 4 Student 2, use with Activity 21 on page 49.

21 **Ask and answer.** Ask your partner one question. Respond to your partner's question with the correct answer from the list below. Take turns.

Questions:
1. Will anyone watch the rocket launch on TV tomorrow?
2. Why does no one want to communicate with us?
3. Does everyone want people to travel in space?
4. Will someone in your family be an astronaut?

Answers for your partner:
a. Someone may want to go, but the trip takes many months.
b. We may all be able to see it if the sky is not cloudy.
c. Luis may know because he likes to study the solar system.
d. It must have an atmosphere like Earth's.

Unit 5 Student 2, use with Activity 16 on page 59.

16 **Ask and answer.** Respond to your partner's question with the correct answer from the right. Then ask your partner a question about a picture on the left.

a

what kind / cloth / weave

1

b

what / family tradition / pass down

2

My Words

Word	Picture
Word in my language	

Word	Picture
Word in my language	

Word	Picture
Word in my language	

Word	Picture
Word in my language	

Word	Picture
Word in my language	

Word	Picture
Word in my language	

My Words

Word	Picture
Word in my language	

Word	Picture
Word in my language	

Word	Picture
Word in my language	

Word	Picture
Word in my language	

Word	Picture
Word in my language	

Word	Picture
Word in my language	

My Words

Word	Picture
Word in my language	

Word	Picture
Word in my language	

Word	Picture
Word in my language	

Word	Picture
Word in my language	

Word	Picture
Word in my language	

Word	Picture
Word in my language	

Unit 1
stickers

Unit 2
stickers

TRUE

TRUE

TRUE

TRUE

TRUE

FALSE

FALSE

FALSE

FALSE

FALSE

Unit 3
stickers

Unit 4
stickers

Unit 5

stickers

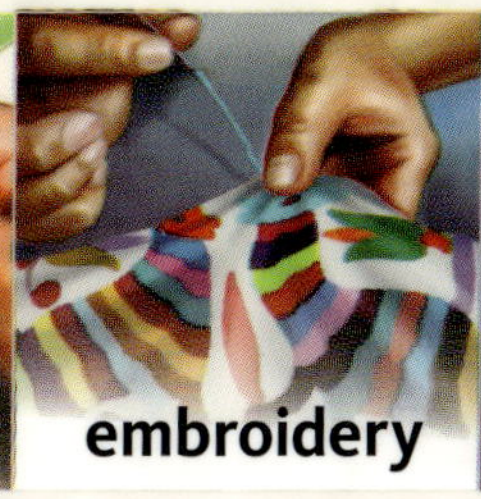